India's Search
for National
Identity

BY THE SAME AUTHOR

Charles Grant and British Rule in India
Muslim Civilization in India (Editor)
The Hindu Tradition (Editor)
Pakistan's Western Borderlands
Encyclopedia of Asian History (Editor-in-Chief)

India's Search for National Identity

(Revised Edition)

WITHDRAWN

Ainslie T. Embree

With an Introduction
by
Eugene Rice

Chanakya Publications
Delhi

ISBN : 81-7001-032-2

INDIA'S SEARCH FOR NATIONAL IDENTITY
by
Ainslie T. Embree

Copyright © 1980 Ainslie T. Embree

First Hard-Cover Edition : 1980
Second Revised Edition : 1988
by
CHANAKYA PUBLICATIONS
F-10/14 Model Town, Delhi 110009

Cover Design : O.P. Sharma

Printed in India by
Ashoka Printers
17, Sri Nagar Colony
Delhi 110052

Preface to the Revised Edition

The original version of this book was written in India at a time when great changes were taking place in the political system, as there are at the present time when it is being republished. It seemed to me then, as it does now, that beyond those changes were the enduring patterns of a dynamic society characterized by an ability to fit incongruous and discordant elements into an immensely complicated mosaic. Accounts of India often stress that it possesses an ancient civilization with a remarkable ability to absorb other cultures. This is to some extent a misleading reading, for while India has, of course, a very ancient past, what has endured is not so much material artifacts, splendid though so many of them are, as ideas, values, and customs. Foreigners are sometimes astonished at how new, almost impermanent, the cities of India are, in comparison with, say, the old cities of Europe. That the survivals of the past are in the lives and consciousness of the people is part of the fascination of India, but it means that more than most countries, India lives always with the heavy burden of the past. And to emphasize that India has absorbed other cultures is to miss a fact of enormous significance for modern India : other cultures were not absorbed, but they continued to exist side by side with each other and with the dominant culture. What was produced was not a synthesis but patterns of culture quite unlike those that developed elsewher in the world. Modern history has introduced peculiar stresses into the fabric of those patterns, and this essay attempts to trace the development of some of these, particularly those having to do with the contradiction between claims for representative government based upon an aggregation of individuals and those based upon the claims for group representation. The contradictions in these opposing claims are now visible in many parts of the world, but they had been very little examined in the period when Indian leaders were engaged in their momentous task of defining a nation. In Lebanon, Northern Ireland, and, of course, in India itself, the claims are often made in terms of a religious faith, and while there is no gainsaying its importance, beyond religion is the group, not the nation, as the source of one's identity. For three or four generations before Independence, Indian nationalists asserted the primacy of identification with the nation, not a group.

If India was the first major country to come to terms with those conflicting claims in its search for national identity in the context of foreign rule, so it may be one of the first to find a politically viable solution to a problem that now haunts the world. Even in countries like Great Britain and the United States, with long established political systems based upon the rule of the majority, the claims of minority groups for special recognition challenges the theory and practice of representative government as it developed in the nineteenth century.

This book, then, is not so much a history of modern India as an interpretation of that history during a period when a nationalist ideology was being formulated in the context of foreign political domination and the conscious reassertion of indigenous values and traditions. Concentration on this theme has meant that many aspects of modern Indian life have been either ignored or touched upon very lightly and that most attention has been given to political events and decisions. The assumptions, that underlie much of the book are sketched in the first chapter. One is the importance of the creation of a modern structure of administration for the development of the complex of ideas that we call nationalism ; another is the crucial role, particularly significant in India, of leaders whose personal identities became involved with the quest for nationality. Many of the questions asked about Indian nationalism have arisen out of the European historical experience, and it is hoped that, while Indian nationalism is illuminated by these questions, they will in turn suggest questions about the origins and development of nationalism elsewhere.

This book was written with a specific audience and purpose in mind : to provide American university students, who were not specializing in South Asian Studies, with materials for a comparative study of nationalism. It has been found useful for that purpose, and I am pleased that Chanakya Publications are making it available once more. The details that were included for the previous audience will be familiar to Indian readers, but it is hoped that this attempt to interpret nationalism in South Asia in a way that will invite comparison with nationalist movement elsewhere may be of interest to them.

In the preface to the original edition. I noted that in writing even a small book, one occurs many debts of gratitude, but I especially recorded my thanks to old friends : B.R. Nanda, V.C. Joshi, Sourin Roy, and Sugata Dasgupta. They are thanked once more, and, in addition, all those other friends in India who through the years have helped me through both agreeing and disagreeing with my ideas. As editor of a series on nationalism in which this book first appeared, my colleague, Professor Eugene Rice of Columbia, provided an introduction which set its themes in a larger context of modern world history ; and it is republished here with its vivid reminder that "for good or ill the world has begun to live a single history."

Columbia University
November 1987

Ainslie T. Embree

Introduction
by *Eugene Rice*

One of the intellectual virtues of our time is a willingness to recognize both the relativism of our own past and present beliefs and the civilizing value of the study of alien cultures. Yet, in practice, as every teaching historian knows, it is immensely difficult to construct a viable course in world history ; and almost as difficult to include satisfactorily unfamiliar, and especially non-Western, materials in the traditional Western Civilization survey course. The reason for this difficulty is that until very recently mankind had no common past. The pre-Columbian civilizations of America attained their splendor in total isolation from the rest of the world. Although the many different ancient peoples living around the Mediterranean were often in close touch with one another, they had little knowledge about civilizations elsewhere. The Chinese knew accurately no other high civilization. Until the nineteenth century, they regarded the ideals of their own culture as normative for the entire world. Medieval Europe, despite fruitful contact with the Islamic world, was a closed society ; medieval Western historians identified their own past with the history of the human race and gave it meaning and value by believing that this past was the expression of a providential plan.

The fifteenth-century European voyages of discovery began a new era in the relations between Europe and the rest of the world. Between 1500 and 1900, Europeans displaced the populations of three other continents, conquered India, partitioned Africa, and decisively influenced the historical development of China and Japan. The expansion of Europe over the world gave Western historians a unifying theme : the story of how the non-Western world became the economic hinterland, political satellite, and technological debtor of Europe. Despite an enormouly increased knowledge of the religions, arts and literatures, social structures, and political institutions of non-Western peoples, Western historians wrote a universal history that remained radically provincial. Only their assumptions changed. Before 1500, these assumptions were theological ; by the nineteenth century, they were indistinguishable from those of intelligent colonial governors.

The decline of European dominance, the raise to power of hitherto peripheral Western countries such as the United States and the Soviet Union and of non-Western ones such as China and Japan, and emergence of a world economy and a state system embracing the planet have all created further options and opened wider perspectives. Historians of the future will be able to write real world history because for good and ill the world has begun to live a single history ; and while this makes it no easier than before to understand and write the history of the world's remoter past, contemporary realities and urgencies have widened our curiosity and enlarged our sympathies and made less provincial our notions of what is relevant to us in the world's past.

One viable way to overcome the ethnocentric provincialism of an exclusively Western perspective is to deal with both Western and non-Weastern civilizations on a comparative basis. The comparative procedure has a double advantage. On the one hand, it describes a culture different from our own and makes clear to us that in order to understand it we must scan its history with humility and sophistication, abandoning implicit analogies with our own civilization and leaving aside some of our most fundamental assumptions about time, space, causality, and even about human nature itself. On the other hand, it encourages us to make explicit those very assumptions of our own tradition we now recognize to be different or unique. By studying comparatively an alien civilization we learn something about it—a good in itself—and at the same time sharpen our understanding of ourselves.

Professor Embree's book serves these purposes admirably, for it is at once an excellent introduction to the modern states of India and Pakistan and a fascinating study of how nationalism has flourished in a non-Western setting. In 1880 India had no physical, political, social, religious, or linguistic unity ; and it was ruled by foreigners. In 1947 the entire subcontinent—not one of whose many languages, Gandhi once remarked, had a word for "independence" intelligible to the masses—was free of foreign rule, free and independent, but not united. For in India the heady consciousness of national identity had spread in a society that attached primary importance to religious identification. Nationalism therefore accentuated rather than minimized the division of Hindu and

Muslim and produced not a single nation state, but two : India and Pakistan. Professor Embree's account of India's search for national identity between 1880 and 1947 is rich in irony and instruction. He gives us important comparative evidence about nationalism : what it is and how it works. The Indian experience he describes helps explain the relation between a growth of national sentiment and the progress of administrative unification and between nationalism and political ideology, allied at one time and place with the struggle for civil liberty, at another to militarism and reaction. The Indian experience makes us see more familiar stories of national unification, those of nineteenth-century Germany and Italy, for example, in a new and fruitful perspective. And finally, the Indian experience underlines one of the critical paradoxes of contemporary history : the diffusion of doctrines, which have come to seem to many Europeans and Americans to be symptoms of disease in the body politic rather than of health, among non-Western peoples who have made them the novel foundation of their sense of individual dignity, a call for social revolution, and the hope and motor of movements of national liberation around the globe.

Eugene Rice

Columbia University

For Sue

Contents

1
One Great
Nation ?

In 1888 Sir John Strachey, one of the ablest of the British administrators of India in the nineteenth century, with an excellent knowledge of the country's political and social history, made this judgment:

> This is the first and most essential thing to learn about India— that there is not, and never was an India, or even any country of India, possessing, according to European ideas, any sort of unity, physical, political, social or religious . . . That men of the Punjab, Bengal, the North-Western Provinces, and Madras should ever feel they belong to one great nation, is impossible.[1]

Not only was he responding to a nascent nationalist movement which he regarded as a threat to the system of law and order he had helped to create, but also he was expressing a genuine conviction based upon what seemed to be an unbiased reading of the obvious facts of Indian history. On the basis of the same facts, but from a different perspective, the great Victorian reformer John Bright had argued thirty years earlier that the lack of any common nationality within India would prevent the endurance there of British rule. He believed that a country with twenty different nations and twenty languages could never be consolidated into one compact and enduring empire.

What these observers were emphasizing was that India lacked the elements generally regarded as the essential ingredients of nationality: a common language, a common religious tradition, and a historical experience shared by the majority of the people. India seemed, in fact, to be peculiarly fragmented precisely where unity and cohesion were demanded. Although Strachey and the others may prove to be right in the long run, they were mistaken in their belief that nationalism in the nineteenth century depended upon the cultural homogeneity characteristic of England or France. The variety and complexity of the manifestations of nationalism throughout the world have prevented any wholly satisfactory generalizations to explain this phenomenon, but one feature that does appear to be common to the development of nationalism in many countries in the prior creation of a modern structure of administration. This is the point made by Carl Friedrich when he asserts, after a survey of the growth of nationalism, "the building of the state comes first, and it is within the political framework of the state that the nation comes into being, or at any rate to fruition."[2] In this analysis, the modern state, with its mechanisms for organizing and controlling social activity, is seen as the producer, not the product, of nationalism.

Origins of Indian Nationalism

This insight has special relevance to the Indian situation, where nationalists reject as a reflection of Western chauvinism the argument that their nationalism is a Western import, unknown before British rule. They are correct, insofar as a nationalist movement necessarily draws its inspiration and vitality from the indigenous cultural tradition. But British rule did contribute that pattern of administrative organization characterized as "Western" or "modern." This political modernization was the base in India for the development of the variegated and powerful sentiments that make up what we call "nationalism."

Benjamin Disraeli defined a nation as "a work of art and a work of time," gradually created by "a variety of influences—the influence of original organization, of climate, soil, religion, laws, customs, manners, extraordinary accidents and incidents in their history and the individual character of their illustrious citizens."[3] Out of such forces came the dominant political idea of modern times: The nation, however defined, is the highest and most natural form of social organization, demanding complete allegiance from all those who live within its territorial boundaries and taking precedence in its claims over such other centers of loyalty as religious institutions, class, and family. The groups of people constituting the nation are regarded as bound together in a common destiny. In the nineteenth century constitutional government and representative institutions were generally accepted as the political forms most conducive to national well-being; but transcending the commitment to any particular political pattern was always the emphasis on the uniqueness inherent in being German or American or French.

One new and supremely important political consequence of this definition of the state in terms of nationality was the insistence that the rulers and the ruled should share a common nationality. In India's past, as in the rest of the world, the rulers frequently had been alien in culture and race. A related characteristic of nationalism of significance for India in the late nineteenth century was the sense that "individual identity hinges on the existence of a national identity."[4] The leaders in the search for nationhood identified their own needs and aspirations with those of the society as a whole. In the beginning of a nationalist movement there may be great disparity between the aspirations of the leaders and of the masses, which was the case in India, as the British never wearied of pointing out. But the triumph of nationalism comes when the masses share some of the sense of correlation between national and personal identity.

In the second half of the nineteenth century the nationalist sentiment then operating so powerfully in Europe became part of the thinking of important segments of the Indian intelligentsia. The national movements that had ended in the unification of Italy and Germany were well known to them, and Mazzini's writings were popular in translations in both English and Indian languages. Such analysts of the political process as John Stuart Mill, Herbert Spencer, and Auguste Comte were familiar to the intellectuals in the great new urban centers of Bombay, Calcutta, and Madras, and the intellectuals had memorized in school Shakespeare's patriotic speeches and Milton's defense of political liberty. English literature and European history thus provided Indian nationalists with their illustrations and metaphors. Using European models, they created out of India's past what John Stuart Mill called the strongest cause for the rise of a sense of nationality: "the possession of a national history, and consequent community of recollections, collective pride and humiliation, pleasure and regret, connected with the same incidents in the past."[5]

The development of such a sense of nationality was everywhere complex and haphazard, but there were especially complicating factors in the Indian situation. One factor was that the changes in political institutions and the whole process of national unification had to take place in the context of a vital traditional society whose economic and social structures were different or in a different stage of development from those in which European nationalism had flourished. The other was the inescapable fact that the instrument of political transformation was an alien government.

Many attempts have been made to analyze the effects of British rule on India, but, whether the judgments are friendly or harsh, they have often been misleading because of the assumption that British rule in India is a component that can be isolated from the fabric of Indian society. British rule and Indian nationalism both were organically related to the society in which they operated, and the antithesis often made between them is false. As already emphasized, the apparatus of the modern state was the framework that made the growth of nationalism possible, and in India this framework was provided by the administrative structures created by the British. British rule was, in the common phrase, "imposed" on India, but its manifestations—political, social, and economic—were inextricably blended into Indian life. The technology, commercial methods, and political institutions introduced into India were British or, at least, Western; but once they were accepted by large segments of the Indian population, they ceased to be "British" and became simply aspects of modernity shared by India and the rest of the world. At the same time there were many levels of Indian life, especially those relating to religion and the family, that were scarcely touched by the Western intrusion.

Because of the mingling of modern and traditional elements, the search for national identity in India is marked by paradoxes and ambiguities that make possible conflicting interpretations of its historical development. The struggle for independence against an alien invader can be seen as the dominant theme, with emphasis on the dynamic role of the Indian National Congress from its founding in 1885 to the moment of triumph in 1947 when India became free. It is also possible to read the story as the classic example of Western imperialism, with India's agricultural resources serving the ends of capitalistic, industrialized Great Britain. Or Hindu-Muslim tensions can be seen as the central motif of the period, with the partitioning in 1947 of the united India created in the nineteenth century as the proof of an irreconcilable division within the social fabric. From a quite different standpoint, modern Indian history may appear as an exercise in Western trusteeship. The growth of constitutionalism and responsible government is, in this version, not the achievement of the nationalist movement but of British administrators and civil servants.

All these interpretations deal with the same sets of facts, and they share an overestimation of the uniqueness and the power, for good or evil, of the British presence in India. What is important is not that the rulers were British, but that they were the bearers of the institutions of political modernization. The specific concern of this book is the interaction of these institutions with an increasingly articulate expression of nationalist sentiment underlying modern Indian history.

Profile : 1880s

Almost any point in the nineteenth century could be chosen for a starting point of an examination of this process of interaction. In the very early years Ram Mohan Roy (1772-1833) and others in Calcutta saw the advantages that might accrue from an intellectual association with the British, who were "advocates of liberty and promoters of knowledge."[6] Or 1835 is symbolic as the point at which the government began to support the use of English as the medium of higher education. This meant that English, not an Indian language, was to be the vehicle of Indian nationalism. Somewhat like Latin in the Middle Ages in Europe, English was to be the language of the learned, providing a common medium of expression for people with diverse linguistic backgrounds. It also made accessible to India the ideas of the West, including nationalism itself. The uprisings of 1857 are also a landmark as an unsuccessful attempt by representatives of the old political and social order to overthrow the new power. But 1880 has been chosen for the purposes of this study because by that time the political, economic, and intellectual forces of both British power and traditional Indian society had interacted to produce a society that had many of the characteristics of the modern nations of the Western world

and that differed sharply from preceding Indian political structures.
A rough profile of India in the 1880s is perhaps the best way to
illustrate this.

Administration: By 1880 all of the Indian sub-continent had
been brought under either the direct control of the central government located in Calcutta or indirect control through Indian rulers
who acknowledged the supremacy of the British crown. Although
direct rule was exercised in only three-fifths of the area, that area
included almost four-fifths of the population, all the great cities, the
seaports, and the Indo-Gangetic plains, one of the most populous
and fertile regions of India. Beyond India proper, the government
of India controlled such outposts as Aden on the Arabian coasts
and, by the end of the decade, the whole of Burma. Throughout
this vast area there was not then, or indeed at any time, unbroken
peace. But what impressed observers was the general stability of the
region. To a considerable degree this was the result of the physical
force that the government of India was able to apply, but it also
indicated wide-spread acceptance of British rule. For the British it
was this passive acceptance that sanctioned their rule, making them
the legitimate successors of the previous rulers.

The major instruments of the government's power were the
army and the civil bureaucracy. The Indian army had about
200,000 men, of whom 60,000 were British, the rest Indian. There
were about 2,000 officers of commissioned rank—all British. In
1880, by the standard of contemporary European armies, it was
neither very efficiently organized nor well armed; but in the Indian
context, both in relation to the neighbouring countries and to any
possible internal armed uprising, its superiority was axiomatic. The
factors that had given the British their military success for a century still obtained; modern weapons, discipline, mobility, and
efficient arrangements for military supplies. Perhaps the most important difference between the Indian army in 1880 and that of any
earlier Indian ruler was that the army was under direct and immediate control of the central authority. Lack of such control previously had allowed local officials and military commanders to
build up centers of power to be used against central administration.
Furthermore, while army officers frequently occupied high posts in
the Indian bureaucracy under the British, especially in the early
period, the principle of civilian control was never seriously challenged. The civilian anthorities were the rulers of India, and the army

was their instrument, never their master. The army was part of the governmental structure, performing a defined role; it was not a potential rival for political power.

In 1880 the location of that power in India was without question the governor general and the Indian Civil Service. While ultimate authority was vested in the British crown, India was governed from Calcutta, not London. The principal function of the home government was not to direct the administration itself, but to evaluate actions taken by the Indian governments and to guide those governments in their future actions. The government of India to a large degree was autonomous, functioning at all levels in much the way any government would have, given the suppositions and powers of its particular ruling class.

The bureaucratic structure of this government, however complicated in detail, was relatively simple in outline. At the top were the governor general and the six members of his council, appointed by the British crown. For legislative purposes this council was enlarged by twelve members appointed by the governor general, two or three of whom were Indians. The powers and functions of this legislative body were very modest, but despite all disclaimers by the British, it was regarded by an increasing number of Indians as foreshadowing a parliamentary structure, and the line of development between the present Indian parliament and the Legislative Council is direct and unmistakable. Much of the power of the central government was delegated to provincial administrations. There were seven of these, differing somewhat in organization, but in general duplicating the central structure, with a governor, an executive council, and a legislative council. The provinces were in turn divided into districts, each with a population of about a million people.

The actual work of administration, whether at the central, provincial, or district level, was in the hands of the Indian Civil Service, a body very different in power and composition from the civil services of other governments. The Indian Civil Service in 1880 had only about one thousand members, of whom all but a half dozen or so were British. Since they held all the key administrative posts—including the crucial positions of collectors, as the heads of districts were usually known—the civil servants, not the governor general, were the real rulers of India. With their long tenure, superior knowledge of the administration, and a very strong

awareness of their indispensability to the maintenance of British
power in India, they had a kind of power not enjoyed by many
other ruling groups in the nineteenth century. It was in recognition
of its position in the power structure that the early nationalist
leaders made admittance of Indians to the Civil Service a central
part of their demands. In 1880 Indians were not formally barred
from the Civil Service, as they had been at any earlier date, but
racial prejudice combined with educational restrictions to prevent
the entry of any but the most gifted and the most persistent.

Although the government of India in the 1880s was a des-
potism, its functions were limited, and it did not seek to bring
about any widespread social or economic changes. As far as social
change was concerned, one of the conclusions the British in India
had drawn very early, and which had been reinforced by the uprisings of 1857, was that it was best not to attempt to interfere in
social and religious customs. For this reason, the government of
India was even less innovative in the second half of the nineteenth
century than it had been in the first half. The general assumption
that the Indians did not care who ruled them, provided they were
left undisturbed in their customary ways of life, made for a profoundly conservative attitude on the part of officials. In the economic sphere, however, the government's policy was more
ambiguous. It was notably active in the creation of the whole
new system of communications, and irrigation projects opened up
new areas for agriculture and increased yields elsewhere.

In outline, this structure of administration does not differ
radically from that of the Indian empire of the Turkish Mughals ;
the territorial divisions, especially at the local level, were often
identical with divisions of the Mughal provinces, and the functions
of the officials were also analogous. Indeed, the basic pattern was
the one used by the Mauryas in the third century B.C. and by
successive imperial rulers. The British themselves were fond of
making this analogy, perhaps because it gave a kind of historical
legitimization to their rule. But there were differences that were
more important than the similarities, and it was these that helped
to make India in the 1880s a modern state, with unique possibilities of development.

Communication : One difference has already been stressed in
connection with the army : the control exercised by the central
authority. The possibility of such control was in large measure

the product of the technological achievements in communication that occurred, quite fortuitously, with the expansion of British power in India. The importance of the railway and telegraph were recognized almost at once by the government of India, and by the 1880s India had a remarkably complete communications system. Railways linked the interior of the country to the seaports; the Grand Trunk Road stretched from Calcutta to Lahore; telegraph lines reached into areas served by neither railways nor good roads; and an efficient postal service operated almost everywhere. We have no studies analyzing in detail what this rapid expansion of new systems of communications meant for India, but it must have made people in different parts of the country aware of each other and their common interests, thus providing a base for building a sense of nationality. There is a measure of irony in this, since the Brirish officials responsible for these changes insisted on the impossibility of unity among India's people.

Economy : The centralization of political power and the general improvement in communications made it profitable for the first time to transport agricultural products to distant areas within India as well as to foreign markets. India had been a center of trade since time immemorial, but the goods involved had been mainly those classifiable as luxury items, light in weight and small in bulk, such as spices, textiles, indigo, and ivory. The basis of the new trade was entirely different. By 1880 wheat was one of India's main exports, with the farmers of Punjab no longer raising crops only for local consumption, but also for a competitive world market. Other products, including hides, jute, raw cotton, tea, oilseeds, and rice, experienced the same expansion.

Throughout this period India had a favorable balance of trade exporting far more than she imported; for example, in 1883 the value of exports exceeded imports by 186 million rupees. Most of the imports were manufactured goods; nearly 80 percent of them came from Great Britain. This excess of raw material exports over imports became a central theme in the Indian nationalist interpretation of the effect of British rule on India, the argument being that India was drained of her natural wealth to support the industrial power of Great Britain. Although the argument in this form needs qualification, there can be little doubt that the emphasis in the late nineteenth century on the production of agricultural products for export to foreign markets, as well as to new markets within India itself, profoundly affected the course of India's economic development. The increase in external trade alone, aside from internal trade developments, which were probably equally great, was very large—about eightfold since 1800. But this was not reflected, as might have been expected, in the growth of industrialization or large-scale urbanization. India continued overwhelmingly to have an agricultural economy, but one that was open to the influence of world markets.

Population Growth : Changes in the size and distribution of the population that were clearly visible by 1880 also underscored the transformation taking place in economic and political structures. Although the evidence is admittedly fragmentary, it is estimated that the Indian subcontinent had a population of about 100 million in the first century A.D. and that growth was very slow until 1800, when the figure was about 125 million. There were undoubtedly fluctuations within this period, both over the whole area and within different regions, but no radical changes seem to have taken place until the nineteenth century. The population growth then accelerated, slowly at first, rapidly after 1850; and when the first census was made in 1871 there was a population of about 250 million. Although this was an enormous increase in absolute terms, the growth rate was not higher than that of many other areas of the world, including Europe, in the nineteenth century. What is of greatest importance is that population growth took place not in the context of industrialization and urbanization as in Europe, but in an economy that was still overwhelmingly agricultural and rural. Of the total population in 1881, 9 percent was urban, and this proportion had probably not changed much since 1800. But if the degree of urbanization had not altered, the location and function of the great cities had changed radically. The three largest cities—Bombay, Calcutta, and Madras—were all new; two hundred years before they had been at best small villages. Delhi, Agra, Lahore, the great court cities of the Mughals, probably had fewer inhabitants than they had in the seventeenth century and they had lost their old importance. The new cities were, almost without exception, centers of trade and industry. They were also centers for the law courts and educational institutions, two other aspects of change that marked off the new India from the old and helped to define her as a nation state.

Law : In the nineteenth century most British officials would have argued without hesitation that the greatest change that had been brought about by British control in India was the introduction of what they liked to call the "rule of law." The suggestion implicit in this claim—that before the coming of the British India did not have a system of law —is obviously untenable, since no civilization could survive without a framework of law. Nevertheless they were probably correct in their general assessment of the importance of the system of law they have introduced. The innovative influence of the new system came from both the laws promulgated by various legislative bodies and the law courts where they were administered. A remarkable change had taken place in that for the first time there was a large body of legislation applicable everywhere in India and actually enforced. This law was universal both in the sense that it was effective throughout British India (but not in the Indian states) and that it had equal application to all citizens, irrespective of civil or religious status. Both the criminal and commercial codes were based wholly on Western law, with little in them to suggest any kind of continuity with India's past. The Evidence Act of 1872 completed the process of making all aspects of legal procedure conform to British practice. The Western origin of so many of the laws, combined with their universality of application, moved Indian society away from some of its traditional moorings.

A very important exception in regard to the universalization of law was made, however, in regard to personal law, that is, in areas relating to such matters as marriage, divorce, adoption, and inheritance. Here, in line with the general principle of not interfering in religious customs and beliefs, laws were applicable according to the religious group to which a person belonged. This made for an extremely complicated legal systen, for the nature and possibilities of divorce proceedings would depend, for example, on whether one was Hindu, Christian, or Muslim. The Government was, in effect, enforcing through law the customs of particular religious communities. This practice had its analogue in that of Western countries, including Great Britain, where it was assumed that the divorce laws reflected Christian beliefs. There were, however, a number of differences in the Indian situation. The government was not only legalizing a variety of belief systems, but within those systems, particularly in the Hindu but also, although to a lesser extent within the Islamic, there was no recognized consensus on such matters. There does not seem to have been much discussion of the advisability of the diversity of personal law at the time, or a recognition that a modern nation-state would move towards the demand for a common personal law for all its citizens. That the existence of a variety of personal laws should have been so readily accepted in the 1880s but became a subject of intense of and divisive debate in the 1880's illustrates one of the transformations made by the formulations of a nationalist ideology and the difference between an imperialist political power and a nation-state.[7]

But no matter what kind of legal case was involved—criminal, commercial, or religious—the system of courts in which they were heard was one that was derived from Western practice. Perhaps in no other area of Indian life was so complete an institutional change affected as in the judicial process, with its network of courts extending from the high courts in each of the provinces, through civil and criminal district courts, down to local courts. These courts, with their common body of law, their uniform procedures, and their interlocking structures, were an integral ingredient in the process of making a social change, although the nature of that change is not without great ambiguity. On the one hand, the use of precedents in the law courts probably tended to give customs that had been purely local and perhaps of no great antiquity, the status of law, and so to make for greater rigidities in Indian society ; on the other hand, the possibility of getting a decision through a court of law made it possible to introduce new conventions into the society. Cases dealing with the position of castes in the society provide examples of both, with groups going to court to claim higher status than had traditionally been accorded them. The courts dealt with many matters of this kind which in British courts would not have been considered legal issues.

Education : By 1880 important changes had also taken place in the field of education. India had had its own systems of education for the transmission and preservation of the traditional culture, but in the nineteenth century new content and new institutional forms were introduced. In general, as in the case of the legal system, the direction was towards uniformity and universality so that curricula and methodologies were remarkably similar throughout India. This was apparently as true of government schools where the medium of instruction was an Indian language as it was of those where the medium was English.

Universities modeled on the University of London, that is, a parent examining body for numerous teaching colleges, had been established in Calcutta, Bombay, and Madras in 1857. The universities themselves were government-sponsored, but the colleges were operated by both government and private interests, often foreign missionary societies and churches. English was the medium of instruction for higher education, and the curriculum was almost wholly Western in content : European history, English literature, and Western philosophy. An important aspect of this western-oriented curriculum was that it was believed by many of those responsible for it that it would communicate not only factual knowledge but that in itself western learning, particularly English literature, would have an elevating effect on the morals of the students.[8] In government institutions as well as in missionary ones, it was fondly hoped that exposure to the great literature of the West would weaken the hold of Hinduism and Islam on the lives of the students and lead them to an acceptance of true religion. Actual conversions even in missionary schools were extremely rare, but that English literature, including the Bible, was shaping the thinking of Indian intellectuals by the 1880's seems clear from their writings.

Primary and secondary schools were neither free nor everywhere available. As with the colleges, they were operated partly by official bodies and partly by private groups, among which foreign missionary organizations were most conspicuous for the number and quality of their institutions. The regional languages were used in the schools, but a knowledge of English was mandatory for everyone who sought university admission.

Any analysis of the impact and penetration of education into the fabric of Indian society is at best impressionistic because of the lack of suitable data, but the census materials for 1881 and 1891 provide some clues as to what was happening. One familiar fact is the very high rate of illiteracy : 95 per cent of the population in the 1881 census was unable to read or write. But this figure is misleading because it conceals facts of profound importance for the social and political history of India. One of these was the literacy differential between men and women. Over the age of twenty-five,

14 per cent of the men were literate, but only .47 per cent of the women were. Even more striking were the enormous variations in literacy between different classes and castes. Agricultural workers and artisans, who made up 75 per cent of the population, had a male literacy rate of only about 5 per cent. Groups that can be identified very loosely as "professional" or trade, who made up about 12 per cent of the population, had a male literacy rate of about 27 per cent. Figures for literacy by caste tell a confirming story. The Brahmans in Madras had a male literacy rate of 72 percent ; in Bombay, 65 percent; and in Bengal, 50 percent, despite the fact that large numbers lived in rural areas.

In relation to the total population, the number of people who knew English was negligible, but they were overwhelmingly high caste, urban, and Hindu, with 80 percent of the English-knowing population coming from such groups. Since they provided the leadership at almost every level of national life—in education, in the professions, in journalism, in the bureaucracy itself—their importance is obvious.

Another aspect of educational development of great importance for Indian nationalism was the difference berween the responses of Hindus and Muslims to Western-style education. Overall the differences were not very significant : the Hindus had a literacy rate in the 1880s of slightly less than 5 percent and the Muslims, a little more than 4 percent. But in regard to higher education, which included a knowledge of English, the differences were very striking: the proportion of Hindu students was far greater than the population ratio of Hindus to Muslims. The position is dramatically illustrated by figures from Rajshahi district in northern Bengal. Muslims made up 75 percent of the population, but in the one college in the district 80 percent of the students were Hindus. These figures do not reflect, as has often been suggested, a fundamentally different attitude between the two religious communilies toward the new Western-oriented educational system, but rather the lack among the Muslims of classes, corresponding in size and influence to those of the Hindus, whose livelihood, either in trade and commerce or in government service, had traditionally been dependent on literacy. It was from these classes among the Hindus that the English-knowing, Western-educated groups were drawn.

These figures taken together lead to the inescapable conclusion that the new educational system and the new ideas that went with

it made their impact largely on those classes that had traditionally
been literate in India and had provided leadership in every sphere
of social and religious life. The Western intrusion had not, therefore, led to the creation of new classes or any fundamental shifts in
social power and prestige but had reinforced in most cases the
prevalent pattern of society. ⌜An important exception to this statement is the loss of power and prestige by the Muslim upper classes,
who had lost their place as the dominant political group. But
their position, like that of the British in the nineteenth century, had
always been somewhat artificial, a temporory function of political
power, not an integral part of the structure of society throughout
the subcontinent. Leadership would come, with few exceptions,
from the Hindu upper-caste groups that had always provided it.
The approximately fifteen hundred students per year who received
university degrees of some kind during the 1880s were an infinitesi-
mal percentage of the total population, but they were an important
part of an influential segment, a vital fact that was often missed by
the British officials, who dismissed them as a group so small and
so unrepresentative of the whole population that their views need
not be seriously considered.

   Religion. In drawing this impressionistic profile of India in
1880, only passing reference has been made to religion. The importance of religious attitudes and allegiances in Indian society is a
truism that needs no special emphasis, but it would be misleading
to attribute to religious groups roles that are the same as, or even
analogous to, those in Western society. Within traditional Indian
society one did not identify oneself as a Hindu ; this is a broad
category imposed by outsiders. Instead identity was in terms of a
particular caste or other group within the society. The same pattern was true of the Muslims, who also tended to think of themselves not in the general category of Muslims, but as members of a
particular social class, involvement in which defined to a large
extent the perimeters of social life. One of the changes, however,
that was taking place with considerable rapidity in the 1880s was a
new self-conscious awareness of religious differences and distinctions. This self-consciousness was both a function and a cause of
the nationalist movement, and one of the fundamental changes
observable between the India of 1880 and the India of 1947 is the
increasing importance of what became known as "communalism,"
that is, the definition of social and political interests through

primary reference to religious communities. The largest of these communities was Hindu, although it must be emphasized that this term covers such a range of belief and practice that the general designation at times conceals more than it reveals of the intellectual beliefs and social practices of those sub-sumed under it. About 187 million people were classified as Hindus in 1881, and the second largest group was the Muslims with about 52 million.

A number of factors must be taken into account when discussing the relative size of the religious communities in India in the 1880's in relation to political leadership. One is that, for reasons suggested above, there was a larger Hindu middle class than there was a Muslim one, even though that term must be loosely used for India of the time. That educated members of the middle class have provided leadership for nationalist movements throughout the world is a truism, and India is no exception. Almost by sheer logic of numbers the leadership of Indian nationalism would come then from Hindus. And this middle class Hindu intelligentsia had memories of the past that were peculiarly suited for a nationalist ideology. A fundamental aspect of nineteenth century Indian intellectual history was the discovery of the greatness of ancient India in religion, philosophy, art, and literature, with great symbols of cultural and political unity furnished by the Maurya and Gupta empires. Literature from the 1880's suggests how potent such memories were in providing the framework for a nationalist ideology. The lack of hostility to British ideas, values and institutions on the part of the early Indian nationalists has seemed odd to some observers, but there was no reason to be hostile since many of the nationalist leaders found these same qualities in their own tradition. This may not have been a justifiable reading of the evidence, but the content of historic memories is more important than textual criticism in the making of a nation.

On a more mundane level, another factor that is of importance in looking at the relative size of the religious communities is their distribution throughout India. Hindus were 73 percent of the population as a whole, but they constituted 90 percent of the great province of Madras and only 43 percent of Punjab. Muslims made up 20 percent of the total population, but they were concentrated overwhelmingly in the northwest and northeast, with about 50 percent of the population of Punjab and Bengal being Muslims. Distribution of communal groups, rather than their total numbers, was to become a crucial factor in Indian history.

*   *   *

Such then was India in outline in 1880. The materials for a nationalist ideology were present in the form of well-articulated social institutions, highly sophisticated literary and artistic traditions, and religious systems that provided satisfactory answers to life's hard questions. To these had been added in the nineteenth century many of the necessary forms of a modern nation-state : a well-organized bureaucracy, educational institutions for the transmission of the ideas and values of modernization, and the infrastructure of modern communications. The next stage, an attempt by Indian groups to participate in the political direction of the new state, was entered into hesitantly and without anticipation of the many factors involved in the undertaking. An essential preliminary for such participation was that the Indian groups should be able to state their interests and their demands in terms significant to both Indian society and the British rulers. The formulation of this statement of nationalist aspirations, centering on various political events and drawing vitality from social and religious movements, constituted the essential feature of Indian history in the last two decades of the nineteenth century.

NOTES

[1]Sir John Strachey, *India* (London : Kegan Paul, 1888), pp. 5-8.

[2]Carl Friedrich, *Man and His Government* (New York: McGraw-Hill, 1963), p. 547.

[3]Quoted in Karl W. Deutsch, *Nationalism and Social Communication* (Cambridge: Massachusetts Institute of Technology Press, 1967), p. 21.

[4]Lucian Pye, *Politics, Personality, and Nation Building* (New Haven, Conn.; Yale University Press, 1968), p. 4.

[5]John Stuart Mill, *Representative Government*, quoted tn Deutsch, *Nationalism and Social Communication*, p. 19.

[6]Ram Mohan Roy, *The English Works of Ram Mohan Roy* (Allahabad: Panini Office, 1906), p. xxiii.

[7]Ainslie T. Embree, "Religion and Politics" *in India Briefing, 1987*, edited by Marshall, Bouton, (New Delhi: Oxford University Press, 1987), examines this issue.

[8]Gauri Viswanathan, "The Ideology of Literary Education in British India 1813-1880" (Ph.D. Dissertation, Columbia University, 1985) is a detailed study of this aspect of education.

2

Voices
of India

In his presidential address to the Indian National Congress in 1890, Sir Pherozeshah Mehta reminded his listeners of Thomas Babington Macaulay's prediction in 1833 :

> The public mind of India may expand under our system till it has outgrown that system ; that by good government we may educate our subjects into a capacity for better government ; that having become instructed in European knowledge they may in some future age demand European institutions.[1]

That day had come, Mehta said, because an educated class existed in India that was ready and able to share in the maintenance—not the destruction—of British rule. Since the Congress was the only group that could articulate opinions, its voice was the voice of India. Mehta insisted that educated Indians had "not learnt the lessons of history so badly as to demand the introduction of full-blown representative institutions." What they wanted was participation in the existing structures of the government in order to make that government responsive to the needs of India as they interpreted them.

Lord Curzon opposed this demand of the Indian National Congress to be recognized as the voice of India when his term of office as governor general ended in 1905. He contended that a genuine, articulate public opinion did not exist in India, but only "a manufactured public opinion . . . which was barren and ineffective because it merely represented the partisan views of a clique."[2]

The real Indians were, he concluded, "the Indian poor, the Indian peasant, the patient, humble, silent millions, the eighty percent who subsist by agriculture, and who know very little of policies."[3] Who then spoke for these silent millions ? Underlying all Curzon's rhetoric was the assumption that it was the British rulers of India who knew best the needs of these millions, not the vocal, English-speaking intellectuals whom he contemptuously dismissed as a "microscopic minority."

In quantitative terms Curzon was correct, but he was ignoring the realities of the Indian situation that made this small, articulate minority in fact the traditional spokesmen for India. Early in the nineteenth century Sir John Malcolm, who had helped to consolidate British power in Western India, showed his awareness of a vital aspect of Indian society when he noted that the Brahmans and other high castes, although for ages nominal servants, had been actually the masters of those in power. Because of the dominance of these groups in Indian society, he argued, any serious challenge to British rule would come from them, not from the military tribes, who were turbulent and bold, but too ignorant and superstitious to threaten the British. The accuracy of Malcolm's observation is suggested by the fact that in 1880 almost all the graduates of Calcutta University were from the Brahman and other small high-caste groups that had traditionally assumed leadership in Bengali society.

By and large, members of these groups had played a dominant role in British rule in India throughout the nineteenth century. The actual physical power of the government was based on its army, composed mostly of Indians, and civilian police forces, virtually all of whom were Indian. The highest paid and most responsible jobs in the bureaucracy were held by Europeans, but these numbered, in all kinds of government employment, only about six thousand. The hundreds of thousands of other jobs were held by Indians. It was not force alone that held India, but "the callaboration of Indians who helped to fulfill the purposes of the British."[4] No adverse moral judgment is implied ; all governments, alien or indigenous, despotic or democratic, depend upon groups in the society actively identifying their interests with those of the rulers. In India, aside from the soldiers, these collaborators were the landlords and the commercial groups, especially in the new cities, and above all those who, having been educated in the new schools and colleges, had found careers in government, educational institutions, and the new professions, such as medicine, law, and journalism. The whole orientation of Indian nationalism was determined by the fact that its leadership came from these groups, whose members were involved with the new political and economic order.

Finally, the opposition of these particular groups to the numerous unsuccessful uprisings against British rule is of special importance in assessing their role in articulating a nationalist ideology. The failure of these uprisings, especially those in 1857, had lasting consequences for the development of nationalism. The English-educated, urban elite had supported the Britsh in 1857. They believed that their own future—and the future of India—was bound up with British rule and what it represented. Being protagonists for the social and political changes they saw coming from Western influence, they had no sympathy with the insurgents' attempt to restore such symbols of the past as the Mughal emperor. The British, although their victory reinforced their feeling of superiority, feared another uprising. Public statements do not always make it clear that after 1857 the government was extremely careful not to antagonize any of the groups of north India—the orthodox religious, the landlords, the old ruling groups—that had participated in the uprisings. As late as 1902 Lord Kitchener, the commander in chief, complained that the Indian army was deployed to protect India not from its external enemies, who he was convinced were the Russians, but from uprisings of the people. The other side of this fear of a repetition of 1857 was respect for those groups likely to fight again, and contempt, or at least mild scorn, for the Bengali businessmen and intellectuals who had supported the government during the uprisings. The result was that when the educated, Western-oriented Indian groups began to seek participation in the structures of power at the end of the century, the process of alienation between them and the British rulers was well under way, although still concealed.

First Responses to the West

The first tentative expression of the involvement of the Indian elite had begun very early—almost simultaneously with the consolidation of British power in Bengal. Early in the nineteenth century

many of the distinctive features of the Indian nationalist movement made their appearance : the use of a political vocabulary
infused with religious and moral overtones ; an emphasis on the
social concerns of the urban elite ; and a desire to introduce
Western norms of political and social behavior. The great figure
in this early period is Ram Mohan Roy, an eloquent spokesman
for an interpretation of Indian history and culture that is of great
importance in the intellectual development of modern India. Roy
accepted the harsh criticisms made of many aspects of Hindu
society by Europeans, but he argued that these were the superstitious excrescences of a degraded age. If one returned to the most
ancient sources of Hindu religion, the Vedas, he believed, one
would find a pure morality and simple deistic faith identical with
the highest reaches of Christian thought. Roy and his followers
urged their fellow Hindus to abandon such practices as child marriage; *sati*, the burning of widows on their husbands' funeral pyres;
and the worship of idols. At the same time they encouraged the
spread of Western education, demanding that the government give
its support to the use of English as the medium of instruction in
the new colleges that were being set up at that time, rather than
the classical languages of the Hindus and Muslims—Sanskrit,
Arabic, and Persian.

Roy's ideas were later institutionalized in the Brahmo Samaj,
a quasi-religious society that sought to provide a spiritual home for
those who were dissatisfied with the cultic practices of Hinduism.
It provided an important service in giving Indian intellectuals a
standing ground during the early years of the Western impact, but
it was too apologetic for what it considered the weaknesses of
Indian society and too anxious to make Hinduism conform to
current Western norms to provide a satisfactory rationale for a
nationalist movement.

Other movements met more adequately the need for a national
consciousness to be rooted in a self-confident assertion of its own
virtues. One was the Arya Samaj, founded by Swami Dayananda
Saraswati (1824-1883). According to Dayananda, India had need
of nothing from the West, for her own spiritual inheritance contained all the truths of science and religion. Like Roy he denounced idol worship and other current practices as late superstitions,
but unlike Roy he refused to make common cause with Christianity and Islam. The apologetic note was gone; he did not argue,

as had Roy, that all religions shared a common truth, but rather that religions were as opposed to each other as night and day. Christianity and Islam, he argued, were absurdly superstitious. Much of the appeal of Dayananda's movement came from this positive, self-assertive attack on other religious groups, but he was equally scornful of the practices and customs of orthodox Hinduism, especially the emphasis on caste purity, idol worship, and the treatment of women.

Dayananda has been called "The Luther of India" by his admirers, an appellation which, while it is too enthusiastic in assessing his historical role, aptly describes the vigor of his arguments. He made no direct attack on foreign rule, but instead he castigated the Hindus for their lack of discipline and patriotism, which had led in the past to India's defeat by foreigners. The implication was plain : The cultivation of discipline and patriotism would lead to the revival of India.

The Arya Samaj emphasized that the true Indians were the Aryas, or "the noble ones", the descendants of the ancient peoples who had come into India in the remote past bearing the pure Vedic religion. The Aryas once ruled India, but dissensions led to their destruction and conquest by enemies ; a return to moral purity would mean the restoration of their power. Dayananda found his most receptive audience in the Punjab, probably because there the Hindus were more conscious of themselves as a group, since they were surrounded by Muslims and Sikhs. His message, with its combination of religious reform and patriotic appeal, gave them an incentive to assert their claims for leadership.

Another union of religion and nationalism, very different in tone and spirit from the Arya Samaj, grew up in Bengal in the 1860s and 1870s. Young writers who had been deeply influenced by modern Western literature and political ideas began to express themselves in poetry, plays, and novels. Their themes were often drawn from India's past, especially from stories of the heroic deeds of the Rajput warriors in their battles against the invading Muslims. The casting of Muslims in the role of villains probably did not rise as much from anti-Muslim feelings as from the frustrations of a generation resentful of foreign domination and conscious of its own weakness. An important aspect of the movement was an undertone of religious mysticism, an exaltation of selfless devotion to Kali, the mother-goddess whose cult was widely popular in

Bengal. Kali is a representation of the dark, vital forces of nature, the slayer of demons whose cult involved blood sacrifices and whose worship demanded passionate commitment. The identification of this mother-goddess figure with India, the motherland, was an easy step.

Anti-Muslim sentiment and a passionate religious nationalism found their most influential statement in the novels of Bankim Chandra Chatterji (1838-1894). Possibly he used Muslims as villains in *Anandamath*, his best-known novel, as a thinly veiled allegory in which the British were really intended to take the role of oppressor ; but it seems more likely that his desire for national purity and unity took the form, as in other nationalist movements, of a revulsion against all alien elements in the society. The British could have filled this role, but Chatterji was not anti-Western in the sense that Dayananda was, and he saw Western ideas as having a creative role in Indian life. His combination of Indian religious symbols with Western concepts of patriotism is shown in a striking manner in his famous poem *Bande Matram* in the novel *Anandamath*. One of the characters in the poem invokes the goddess Kali as both deity and motherland.

> Mother, to thee I bow.
> Who hath said thou art weak in thy lands,
> When the swords flash out in twice
> Seventy million hands,
> And seventy million voices roar
> Thy dreadful name from share to share.[5]

The singer went on to tell the hero, a young man, that the way to drive out the intruder is to use the intruder's method— violence. This mystical nationalism, building on concepts deeply rooted in Indian life, is of great importance for modern India. It is often overlooked because of the later emphasis on non-violence in the Gandhian period, but its romantic appeal provides the background for many later developments.

Role of Regional Languages

The social and intellectual ferments that found expression in Bankim Chandra's novels were not confined to Bengali literature.

Throughout India the creation of new forms of literary expression through the use of regional languages was one of the most striking and contradictory developments in the search for national self-identity. The role of English as a unifying and vitalizing factor in the growth of Indian nationalism has rightly been stressed, but probably this new literature in the regional languages was equally significant. Everywhere in India in the nineteenth century the regional languages gained a new vitality and a new prestige. The classical languages—Sanskrit in the older Indian tradition, Persian for the Muslims—had been replaced by English as the official language and as the medium of higher education. But secondary schools were conducted in the regional languages, as was the day-to-day business of local courts. English missionaries in Bengal at the very beginning of the nineteenth century had shown the possibilities of using Bengali prose—a new literary creation—for communication with the masses and had published not only religious works, but also newspapers and other secular works. Newspapers in all the major regional languages soon became commonplace with every city and large town having at least one. None of them had large circulations—around five hundred seems to have been the norm—and many of them were short-lived. But every copy probably reached at least ten people, and their ideas would spread far beyond that number. The newspapers were frequently sharply critical of the government, but the fact that they were in regional languages and often published in obscure places meant that they had a freedom of expression that, as officials frequently complained, bordered on the seditious. In 1878 a government official concluded, after a survey of his district, "the great political fact of the day" was that "a feeling of nationality, which formerly had no existence . . , had grown up", and that the press could now for the first time "appeal to the whole Native Population of India against foreign rulers."[6]

Other forms of literary activity in the regional languages also contributed to this new sense of self-conscious identity about politics and society. Social evils were attacked in plays and novels : histories were written for the first time in the local languages ; poetry expressed a concern with the ordinary life of the time. These trends were visible in a dozen languages, giving a new self-awareness to regional cultures. The persistence of these regions as cultural and political entities constitutes one of the fundamental

facts of Indian historical experience, for they were far more enduring than the great empires.   This modern development ran counter
to the all-India nationalism, just as the possibility of regionally
based political power had always constituted a challenge to imperial structures.   From this point of view, the cultivation and
encouragement of regional literatures in the nineteenth century
were divisive forces that increased the strains on the fabric of
national unity in modern India, as did the identification of religious
symbols with nationalism.   But it is difficult to see how, without
either a religious or a regional emphasis, an Indian nationalism
could have been created that would have had any vitality, for religious and linguistic preferences provided the basis for the emotional
as well as much of the intellectual appeal of nationalism.

Nationalist Organizations

The proliferation of associations and organizations of all kinds
was another crucial aspect of the development of public opinion
and national identity.   The nineteenth-century British pattern of
voluntary public associations to achieve some desired end through
publicity, discussion, and pressure on authorities was taken over
with remarkable success by the Indian elite.   The National Association was formed in 1851 in Calcutta.   It was open to all classes
and creeds, and its aims were "to assert our legal rights by legitimate means" and "to apply for any amendment or reform . . .
either to the Local Government or to the authorities in England."[7]
This was soon transformed into the British Indian Association,
possibly because the word "national" suggested disloyalty to the
regime.   Its aims were modest : Indian representation on the legislative councils that advised the governor general and the provinicial
governors and admission of Indians to the Civil Service.   The
Indian Association, formed in 1876 under the leadership of S.N.
Banerjea, listed among its aims the creation of a strong body of
public opinion and the inclusion of the masses.   It also made a
direct appeal for student membership and support.   The extent of
student response is indicated by an official's complaint that "the
current of opinion among the educated natives of Bengal is . . .
largely swayed by the views held by schoolboys."[8]

In Madras the Mahajana Sabha addressed itself to more
specific issues : the economic condition of the peasants, the working

of social self-government, and the efficiency of the judicial system. In the Bombay Presidency, the Poona Sarvajanik Sabha emphasized the need for Indian representation at all levels of government including members in the British Parliament. Such sentiments are not revolutionary in the sense that they indicate a desire to overthrow the established order by force, but their fulfilment would certainly have undermined the government of India as it was constituted at the time.

Ilbert Bill

Sir Richard Temple, the lieutenant governor of Bengal, surveying the activities of the political associations in 1876, remarked. "they indicate a stir of thought and movement in the national mind."[9] How justified Temple was in his use of the phrase "the national mind" was demonstrated in the early 1880s after the appointment of Lord Ripon as governor general (1880-1884). Ripon was known to be sympathetic on moral grounds with Indian aspirations, but he was also convinced that unless steps were taken to unite their interests with those of the government there would be increasing bitterness and estrangement, making British rule impossible. The reforms that Ripon proposed as a way of granting some measure of participation were moderate, but all were important to Indian public opinion.

The proposed reforms centered on four issues : the Vernacular Press Act, the Arms Act, rules for entrance into the Indian Civil Service, and right of Indian judges to hear criminal cases involving Europeans. The Vernacular Press Act of 1878 had made provision for the censorship of journals published in Indian languages and had been a direct response to the growing criticism of the government in the newspapers that had proliferated throughout the country. The Act had been regarded as an illiberal measure in England as well as in India, as it seemed like such a clear denial of the freedom of speech which was regarded as a hallmark of British life. Ripon's government announced its intention of abandoning the Act, but in subsequent years other administrations had to modify the commitment to a free press. Freedom of the press had been an issue throughout the nineteenth century, and many thoughtful observers argued that a genuinely free press was possible only in a society where the people had the right to change their governors, not in a country

like India where the government's power could not be challenged.
That the press was as free as it was in India is one of the curiosi-
ties of British rule, for far more latitude was allowed to newspapers
than is the case in many independent countries today. The essential nature of Indian nationalism can be explained to a considerable extent by the possibility of public opinion finding expression
even when there were no institutions of responsible government.
The Arms Act, which also dated from 1878, required that all fire-
arms be licensed except those owned by Europeans. One might
have supposed that it would have been of much less interest to
educated Indian opinion, but in fact it was widely criticised by
speakers and writers, many of whom probably had little interest in
either hunting or self-defence. What they found especially distasteful about both the Vernacular Press Act and the Arms Act was
that they revealed a widespread mistrust of Indians dating from the
uprisings of 1857 and a pervasive racism that was increasingly
characteristic of the attitudes of many Englishmen towards Indians.
Racism is not an invention of the late nineteenth century, but
there is no doubt that it finds more frequent expression then than
at any previous time in the relationship between Europeans and
Indians, and it is of peculiar importance in the context of the Indian
demand of participation in political power. So symbolic was the
Arms Act of this racism that Ripon was not able to amend it.
Another issue that was of enormous interest to Indians who had
been educated under the new system of university education were
proposals for changes in the rules governing entry into the Indian
Civil Service, the locus of power within the political structure.
Technically it was possible for Indians to be admitted into the Civil
Service, but since the examinations were given in England, and based
on a wholly British curriculum, the hurdles for Indians were so great
that it is susprising that by the 1880's even a few had managed to
make it. Again, it seems clear that racism and fear of sharing
power with Indians were major factors. So strong was the opposition that even the slight concession of raising the age limit to give
Indian candidates a better chance to prepare for the examinations
could not be made.

The proposed measure of reform that created the greatest
furor was the Ilbert Bill, named after the Law Member who was
its author. The issue was the existing rule that if Europeans were
brought to trial in a criminal court they had the right to be tried

by a European judge. The Ilbert Bill was intended to remove this distinction between British and Indian judges.

From the beginning of his term of office it was apparent that Ripon would be faced with great opposition in his attempts to extend the principles of British liberalism to India. It came from the members of the India Council in London, the advisers of the secretary of state, who were opposed to the liberalism of the Gladstone ministry ; from the Civil Service in India; but overwhelmingly from the British business community residing in India. The Ilbert Bill was the special target of attack. Much was made of the untrustworthiness of Indians and especially the danger confronting an Englishwoman brought before an Indian judge. All of this can be seen as the attempt by a minority to maintain their privileges or as an expression of racism, which indeed it was. But there was more than this involved in the issue : The British community in India was exhibiting what can be thought of as a different sort of nationalism. The British were making claims for themselves as rulers in the same fashion that white settlers in Rhodesia and Algeria have done in our own time. At this time there were only 89,798 Europeans in India, of whom 55,760 were in the army ; but the few thousand businessmen, planters, and professional people manifested a fierce passion against Indian participation in the administration. Much of their anger was directed against the British government for betraying them, and there was even talk of the settlers setting up an independent Indian state, which would be the true guardian of British interests.

In the end the outcry against the Ilbert Bill from the British community was so great that Ripon felt compelled to withdraw it. The Anglo-Indians, as the British residents in India were called, had shown it was possible to control the government of India from India itself as well as from England. This was what an Indian editor had in mind when he thanked the British residents in India "who in one short year taught their Indian fellow subjects that determination and sustained action in support of a cause deeply felt could be invincible."[10]

Indian National Congress

Seen against this background, the decision in 1885 to organize the association that became the Indian National Congress was a

logical expression of the sense of national identity of the Indian
educated classes. The need was obvious for a central organization
of some kind to coordinate the activities of the hundreds of local
associations formed throughout the country to discuss politics and
to mobilize their members for more effective pressure on the
government. From the very start there was a curious sense of
destiny, a belief that the Congress marked a new day in Indian life.
The president of the Congress called it "the first National Assembly
ever yet convened in India," stressing that "not only were all
parts of India represented, but also most classes ; there were bar-
risters, solicitors, pleaders, merchants, landowners, bankers,
medical men, newspaper editors and proprietors ; principals and
professors . . . religious teachers and reformers."[11] A critic might
have noticed the absence of members of the urban working class
or peasants, but then they would also have been absent from any
similar gathering almost anywhere else in the world in 1885. The
Congress was a remarkably representative cross section of educated
India, and that was what it claimed to be.

The successes and failures of the Congress, which has one of
the longest records of continuous existence of any political party
anywhere in the world, are rooted in its origins. Since the beginning its leaders sought not so much a consensus as the identification of issues that would be of interest to a wide spectrum of
opinion, and they endeavored to find a formula that would not
alienate any specific groups. For this reason social reforms did
not occupy a significant place in the Congress' platform. The
complexities of the political society have always been obvious ; the
problem has been to give those complexities an expression that
would present actual possibilities of political action. In 1885 this
involved defining a program that would appeal to the social and
intellectual groups interested in politics, almost all of whom, as
emphasized earlier, were in some sense "collaborationists," in that
they were involved in the new political and economic society associated with British rule in India. They were "modern" men, in
that they preferred the Western, or modern, forms of political institutions to those of traditional India. It was this preference, not
servility, that made Dadabhai Naoroji declare that the Congress,
so far from being a nursery for sedition or rebellion against the
British government, was "another stone in the foundation of the
stability of that Government."[12]

That the nationalists had no desire to replace the political arrangements created by the British with those that had existed previously highlights the ambiguities and dilemmas of Indian nationalism. The nationalists were espousing the values of the foreign rulers' political system, not opposing them. Their criticism of the British was that they had not extended these values in full measure to India. Nor were they as wholehearted in the acceptance of their own past as nationalists often are. Most of them were very critical of many aspects of their society, and their criticisms were frequently the same as those made by Westerners. In addition to this intellectual and emotional acceptance of the value of Western rule, they were convinced that the only way to move toward participation was through granting of their requests by the English, since they did not have the power to demand them or to take them by force.[13]

The resolutions passed by the Indian National Congress in 1885 and at its annual meetings throughout the next ten years sum up the particular concerns of the groups constitutting political India. They asked for an installment of representative government through an increased Indian representation in the legislative councils of the governor general and the governors. They wanted the Civil Service to be made more accessible to Indians through examinations held in India as well as in London. The government's expenditure on military operations outside India and in frontier wars was condemned, but at the same time a plea was made for Indians to have the right to become officers in the army. The poverty of the masses was always stressed with its causes located in the economic policies of the government, especially the high tax on land and the free-trade policy, which deprived Indian industry of all protective duties.

These interpretations of India's needs represented the areas of agreement among the diverse elements for which the leadership of the Indian National Congress spoke. They concealed growing tensions, both in the nationalist movement itself and in the fabric of Indian society. While rooted in Indian social and political life, these were, in the particular forms in which they manifested themselves in the last years of the nineteenth century, the direct product of the Congress' success in creating, however tentatively, a nationalist ideology. Two areas of tension were of immediate concern. One was the result of the emergence of B.G. Tilak (1856-1920) to a position of leadership in the Congress ; the other was the tentative formulation of a rival Muslim nationalism by Syed Ahmad Khan (1817-1898) and other Muslim leaders.

B.G. Tilak

B.G. Tilak's place in modern Indian history is based on his use of religion and regional loyalties as vitalizing forces for the nationalist movement. He was regarded by many of his contemporaries as a reactionary religious revivalist, rejecting the modern world in favor of the world of the past. But in the perspective of nationalist movements elsewhere and of later Indian political life itself, Tilak can be seen as being more open to the forces that were shaping the future than the liberal leaders—men like S.N. Banerjea, Naoroji, and his great rival in Bombay, G. K. Gokhale. Tilak understood, as they did not, that, to be effective, nationalism had to be grounded in the emotions and needs of the people and that it must squarely identify and challenge its enemy.

His main weapon—journalism in Marathi, the language of his region—was the product of the new age, but there were many sides to his crusades to create a patriotism colored by Indian, not Western, assumptions. Striking use was made of the traditional Hindu religious festivals as occasions for patriotic speeches and political education. Tilak saw that these old institutions could be made to serve nationalist aspirations in an effective way. If instead of starting new associations, he wrote, "we give a more or less new turn to the old institutions, then they will in all probability become popular and soon they will be permanent."[14]

This shrewd understanding of the possibilities of using old forms for new political purposes was also seen in his support of the Cow Protection Societies. The cow in India, contrary to the common label, is not regarded as "sacred." She is, however, the symbol and touchstone for many of the deepest emotions of Hindu experience. As a symbol of fertility and of the bounty of nature, the cow was inextricably bound up with religious emotions, becoming not so much sacred, at least in the Western sense, as a mothersymbol. All killing is deprecated in Hindu society, and an orthodox Hindu would see little more reason to kill and eat a cow than to practice cannibalism. The cow was an accessible symbol for Hinduism, which is very amorphous and hard to define. The cow

protection movement was a call to protect Hindu society from its
enemies, who were, in effect, the same as the enemies of the cow—
the British and the Muslims.   The same complex appeal to religion
and sentiment was apparent in Tilak's emphasis on the allegory
of Sivaji, the Maratha chiefta in who had waged a successful war
against the Mughal Empire in the seventeenth century. As Sivaji
drove out the Muslims, so could the Indians drive out the British.

Tilak's nationalism was not only anti-British, it was also by
implication, if not always directly, anti-Muslim.   Emphasis on the
greatness of the past, a common feature of all nationalist movements, meant the Hindu past—a bitterly anti-Muslim past—with
Sivaji as hero.   Such an emphasis in itself would be enough to
create uneasiness or hostility among Muslims, and the proof of this
was the growing number of out-breaks of violence between Hindus
and Muslims.   But aside from this, many Muslim leaders had,
almost from the beginning, regarded the Indian National Congress
as a threat to their own hopes and aspirations.

Muslim Movements

Militant Islam   The rigidities of Islamic intellectual conventions had never precluded intellectual ferment, and a number of
movements of great importance had been at work in the Muslim
community of India long before the formal expression of modern
nationalism.   During the decay of the political power of the
Mughals in the eithteenth century, Shah Wali Ullah (1703-1762)
had sought to unite all Muslims in a common loyalty to their faith.
He emphasized the centrality of the Koranic teachings and traditions that all Muslims shared and stressed the need for religious
unity in a time when political power was no longer a dependable
defense.   His son Shah Abdul Aziz (1746-1824) spelled out the
implications for Muslims of the British conquest. India had ceased
to be Dar-al-Islam, the "Home of Islam," and had become Dar-al-
Harb, the "Home of War," where Muslims could no longer
practice Islam in peace. The duty of pious Muslims was, therefore,
to restore Islam by driving out the non-Muslim rulers. His spiritual successors carried on *jihad*, or holy war, from bases on the
northwest frontier, first against the Sikh rulers of the Punjab, then,
after their defeat, against the British.   While they were not able to
organize an effective challenge to the British, they kept alive a sense

of Islamic separatism and, through nostalgia for past glories, a hope for the future restoration of Islamic rule.

Such Islamic movements were fiercely opposed to any accommodation, political or intellectual, with the new order. Their belief in a return to the primal purity of Islamic faith and their insistence that Islam could only develop in a state where Islamic religion and political power were one made any cooperation with the British impossible. In other contexts a group so firmly grounded in an ideological position might have been expected to serve as a vital organizing force for a nationalist movement that could have challenged foreign rule. They could not fulfill this function in India because of their inability to make any alliances with the other sources of leadership and power within Indian society. The aims of militant Islam had as little place for the liberals of the Indian National Congress as for the extremists of Hindu revivalism. The uprising of 1857 had shown how tenuous were the common interests of the different groups. The failure of the uprisings had further embittered the Muslim leaders and added to their frustrations: Not only were the British secure, but in many areas power was passing to the Hindus, notably to the Bengalis.

Islamic Modernism This leads to a fundamental point for understanding the content and character of the new Muslim nationalism: the change in the position of the Muslims relative to the Hindus. Statistically it is possible to show that in north India Muslims had more than their share of government jobs in proportion to their numbers. But the emotional reality is that the Muslims saw the tide beginning to turn. Public opinion among Muslims represented the views of a small group that realized Muslims everywhere were losing their old positions of leadership. They wanted, in other words, neither proportional power nor parity; they wanted to restore their lost heritage. It is in the complexities of this situation that Syed Ahmad Khan did his seminal work

Syed Ahmad Khan was a member of the old official class of the Mughal Empire. He had entered the service of the British regime as a legal officer, and he gained recognition for his support of the government during the uprisings in 1857. Convinced that the only hope for a tolerable future for Indian Muslims, especially for those of the class to which he belonged, was to come to a reasonable compromise with the British, he tried, on the one hand, to persuade the British that the Muslims were not compelled by religious and historical sentiment to oppose British rule. On the other hand, he tried to persuade the Muslim leadership that they must adjust themselves to the new patterns of administration and government. Both goals could be accomplished by the same method: the acceptance of Western education. This would show the British that Muslims intended to accept the changed conditions of society, and at the same time it would restore Muslims to their place of authority and prestige.

Syed Ahmad Khan argued that such an accommodation entailed no denial of Islamic doctrine. Like Ram Mohan Roy he believed the seeming conflicts between religion and the new learning were caused by corruptions that had been added to the pure original traditions, and a major part of his apologetic was to urge the rejection of many Islamic practices and beliefs then current on the grounds that they did not find support in the Koran. The way to the future was to combine the science of Europe with the learning and culture of Islam. This advocacy of accepting the best of both worlds was institutionalized in the new college he founded at Aligarh, which soon became an important training centre for Muslims who sought freedom from the frustrations of a defeated society through involvement in the new order.

Such freedom was not to be found, Syed Ahmad Khan warned his followers, through participation in the nationalist movement represented by the Indian National Congress. His objection was fundamental: The aims and objectives of the Congress were "based upon an ignorance of history and present-day realities; they do not take into consideration that India is inhabited by different nationalities." These nationalities spoke different languages, professed different religions, followed different customs, and had different historical traditions. This explicit denial of the Congress' faith in one nation carried with it further challenges to the whole nationalist position. He denied that representative political institutions could find root in India's soil, since they were completely alien to her traditions, Hindu or Muslim. India needed a strong, autocratic government to maintain order between the contending nationalities, and this role was admirably fulfilled by the British. Representative rule meant majority rule: the subjection of the Muslim minority to the Hindu majority. But this would lead to suffering for more than the Muslims, for, he said, "they are prone to take the sword in hand when the majority oppresses them."[15]

On the surface Syed Ahmad Khan's deference to the British resembles the Indian National Congress leaders' insistence on their loyalty and devotion, but there is an important difference. Men like Dadabhai Naoroji supported British rule because of their conviction that it promised representative, constitutional government for India. Syed Ahmad had no such vision for India; he was an authoritarian aristocrat, believing in strong paternal rule. A.O. Hume's accusation that Syed Ahmad and his fellows "in their hearts hate British rule"[16] sounds absurd in the light of their almost obsequious praises of the British, but it contains an interesting insight.

In much writing on British rule, it is frequently asserted that the British got along better with Muslims than they did with Hindus, and there is a tedious repetition of the comparison between the "manly" Muslim, especially on the Frontier, and the intellectualized and "effeminate" Bengali Brahman. There is remarkably little evidence, however, from Muslims that they returned this high regard. To take an example from a later stage of nationalism, Jinnah was far more bitter in his comments on the British than was Nehru. Sir Syed in his writings, in a guarded way, sometimes expresses what must have been his own real feeling for the English. He notes that Muslims officials in government service, when they are forced to put up with abuse from arrogant British superiors, exclaim to themselves, "Oh, that I could gain my living otherwise, cutting grass by the wayside were better than this.[17]

The aristocratic class accepted the inevitability of British rule as a political fact, but, consciously or not, they must have hoped for a restoration of Muslim power. Nothing went so certainly against the grain of such a hope as the Congress' demands.

Syed Ahmad Khan's rejection of majority rule had been foreshadowed in a controversy, in which he and other Muslim leaders had long been involved, between Hindi, the most commonly used language of the northern Hindus, and Urdu, the language most commonly used by the Muslims. Urdu was widely used in the law courts of north India, but in 1867 an agitation started for its replacement by Hindi. The argument was that Hindi, written in the Devanagri script, not Urdu, using the Arabic script, was the language known to the majority of the people. The differences between the two languages themselves was not very great, but the two scripts were totally different. Devanagri was associated with Sanskrit and Hindu culture; the Arabic script with Muslim rule and culture. The demand for Hindi was thus part of the general resurgence of Hindu culture, and when the government of Bengal responded by making Hindi the official language in the courts of the Bihar districts, Muslims objected strongly. They saw that more was involved than just prestige: The replacement of Urdu meant loss of employment for Muslims and an increase in the employment of Hindus. Syed Ahmad Khan's conclusion was that "it was no longer possible for the two nations to be partners with each other in any common enterprise."[18]

Traditional Islam A very different approach came from a group of Muslims associated with a school for Islamic studies that had been founded at Deoband, a small town north of Delhi, after the 1857 uprisings. The scholars there maintained a traditional Islamic training that aimed, not at reconciliation with the modern world, but freedom from it. The hopelessness of armed revolt had been demonstrated in 1857, but the alternative was not acceptance of the conqueror. The Deoband school disagreed profoundly with Syed Ahmad Khan and the other modernizers who argued that the salvation of Islam was in rapprochement with the British. For this reason, when Syed Ahmad Khan denounced the Indian National Congress and urged Muslims not to participate in it, the Deoband leaders issued a *fatwa*, a formal statement based on religious law, contradicting him. In secular affairs, it argued, cooperation with Hindus was permissible. Thus a curious situation developed in which the Aligarh group, who followed policies in many ways very similar to those of the liberals who had founded the Congress, were estranged from it, while the traditionalists, so antithetical in their religious and social views, if they did not actually support the Congress, at least did not oppose it. In the end it was the spiritual descendants of the Aligarh movement who favored the creation of Pakistan, while the Deoband group opposed it.[19]

*   *   *

At the end of the century the various internal tensions necessary to a definition of nationality in the Indian context had thus become active, demanding attention and consideration,

Virtually every stand that constitutes the fabric of present-day Indian political life was clearly visible : the "moderates" arguing for compromises phrased according to the vocabulary of Western constitutionalism ; the "extremists" insisting on solutions that recognized the cultural dominance of the Hindu tradition ; and, finally, the anxieties of Muslims, still unfocused, but powerful in their negative statements. All of these reacted to what may be thought of as an external force : the responses of the government of India, and beyond it, the British government. Out of this amalgam came the shifting, uncertain search for nationality in the first two decades of the new century.

NOTES

[1]Pherozeshah Mehta, "Presidential Address," 1890, in *The Indian National Congress* (Madras : G.A. Natesan, 1909 ?), p. 86.

[2]Sir Thomas Raleigh (ed.), *Lord Curzon in India* (London : Macmillan, 1906), pp. 486-487.

[3]*Ibid.*, p. 585.

[4]Anil Seal, *The Emergence of Indian Nationalism* (Cambridge : Cambridge University Press, 1968), p. 9.

[5]Bankim Chandra Chatterji, *Anandamath*, in *Sources of Indian Tradition*, William Theodore de Bary, *et. al.*, (eds.) (New York : Columbia University Press, 1958), pp. 709-714.

[6]Quoted in Seal, *Emergence of Indian Nationalism*, p. 147.

[7]Quoted in B.B. Majumdar, *Indian Political Associations and Reform of Legislature* (1818-1917) (Calcutta : Firma K.L. Mukhopadhyay, 1965), p. 34.

[8]Quoted in Seal, *Emergence of Indian Nationalism*, p. 217.

[9]*Ibid.*, p. 205.

[10]Quoted in Chiristine Dobbin, "The Iibert Bill : A study of Anglo-Indian Opinion in 1883," *Historical Studies : Australia and New Zealand*, Vol. 12 (1965), p. 122.

[11]*Report of the First Indian National Congress Held at Bombay on 28th, 29th, and 30 December 1885*, Lucknow, 1886.

[12]Dadabhai Naoroji, "Presidential Address," 1886, in *The Indian National Congress*, p. 7.

[13]Ainslie T. Embree, "Pledged to India : The Liberal Experiment, 1885-1909," in *The Political Culture of Modern Britain ; Studies in the Memory of Stephen Koss*, edited by Malcolm Bean (London : Hamish Hamilton, 1987), is an examination of the relationship of the Indian nationalist leadership to British Liberalism.

[14]Quoted in Stanley Wolpert, *Tilak and Gokhale* (Berkeley : University of California Press, 1961), p. 68.

[15]de Bary, *Sources of Indian Tradition*, p. 68.

[16]Quoted in I.H. Qureshi, *The Struggle for Pakistan* (Karachi : Karachi University Press, 1965), p. 25.

[17]Sir Syed Ahmed Khan, "The Causes of the Indian Revolt," in *Sir Sayyid Ahmed Khan's History of the Bijnor Rebellion*, translated by Hafeez Malik and Morris Dembo, (East Lansing : Asian Studies Centre, Michigan State University, n.d.) p. 141.

[18]Quoted in Hafeez Malik, *Moslem Nationalism in India and Pakistan* (Washington : Public Affairs Press, 1963), p. 210.

[19]This issue is studied in Barbara Daly Metcalf, *Islamic Revivalism in British India, 1860-1900* (Princeton : Princeton University Press, 1982) and in David Lelyveld, *Aligarh's First Generation : Muslim Solidarity in British India,* Princeton University Press, 1982.

3
Search for
a Center

The first phase of the nationalist movement ended with
challenges to the compromises of the moderates from two direc-
tions : the resurgent Hindu nationalism represented by Tilak and
the Muslim reaction led by Syed Ahmad Khan. The second phase,
from 1898 to 1917, was marked by an increasing articulation of the
tensions within Indian society and, to counter this, a search for
positions that could replace the compromises of 1885. In this
search for a centre the government of India was a more active
participant than it had been in the first period.

In nationalist rhetoric the imperial power is often seen as a
wholly negative force, whose contribution to nationalism is
primarily the provision of an antagonist, compelling the nationalist
leaders to harden their positions and redefine their goals. This view
ignores the creative potential in the existing political structure
actually to shape the form and content of nationalist activity. This
potential existed in India, especially in the period from 1898 to
1917. The first date marks the beginning of the seven-year
administration of Lord Curzon as governor general and the second,
the announcement in August 1917 that Britain's aim in India was
the establishment of responsible government. Within these limits
a number of government actions gave nationalist opinion new
causes and new motivations, but at the same time the political life
of India was subjected to modifications that provided what was in
effect a new framework for nationalist agitations. Some of these
changes, such as the partition of Bengal, are associated primarily
with Curzon's administration, whereas the constitutional reforms

of 1909 reflect the interplay of Indian nationalism, the government of India, and the responses of the British government in London.

Curzon Era

At the end of Lord Curzon's term of office as governor general, a spokesman for the moderate, liberal group in the Indian National Congress, referred to Curzon with distaste as an "Asiatic Viceroy." "He has forgotten English methods of ruling India and is daily growing in love with *Asiatic* ways of ruling . . . This Viceroy will leave the country the most odious and hated."[1] It is curious that an Asian nationalist should denounce a foreign ruler because that ruler was behaving according to the political customs of Asia, not of England, but it is indicative of the orientation of the liberal nationalists.

The irony of Curzon's reputation with the nationalists is that many of the goals for which he had worked were precisely those necessary for a country moving toward nationhood. The record of his administration justifies his claim that his policy had been one of the payment of due regard to Indian authority in the determination of India's needs. Insistence on the autonomy of the government of India led to clashes with the British government in which he was the loser on two notable occasions. One was his assertion of the influence of the government of India over Tibet, which was disavowed by the British government ; the other was his quarrel with Lord Kitchener over the powers of the commander in chief of the army. When he was not supported by the British Cabinet, Curzon resigned, arguing that any weakening of civilian control over the armed forces could lead to military dictatorship.

But in his emphasis on bureaucratic efficiency, Curzon had neither sympathy nor understanding for the nationalist demand for Indian participation in the governmental process. The result was a series of administrative changes that combined with his contemptuous dismissal of Indian democratic aspirations to deepen the growing cleavage between the government and the nationalist leaders. At the same time the reaction to the Curzon policies tended to make more visible the divisions within Indian society itself. Three of these policy decisions were of particular importance in activating Indian political life.

One of these decisions involved the municipal boards set up by Lord Ripon in 1882 to introduce an element of self-government and elected representation to many towns and cities. The boards worked with varying success and often were dominated by government officials, but in the great cities the elected members had gained considerable power. This was especially true in Calcutta, where members of the Indian National Congress were strongly represented. The Calcutta municipal corporation might have justified itself as an exercise in self-government, but Calcutta had already become one of the most unmanageable cities in the world with vast areas of slums unserved by even minimal municipal services. Curzon blamed this on the inefficiency and irresponsibility of the elected members, and in 1899 he had an act passed cutting the elected membership from 66 percent to 50 percent and giving the major share of the power to British officials. The plea of the nationalists that Indians should have a major voice in the government of their own city was answered with quick brutality by a European member of the Legislative Council.

> Commerce made Calcutta. By Commerce I mean European commerce . . . . The history of Calcutta shows it to have been little more than a mud bank until European merchants settled there. The present Bengali population who clamour for the Government of Calcutta are not for the most part natives of the place . . . . The interests of Government and of Foreign Commerce are more important than all other interests put together.[2]

Given this attitude on the part of the Europeans, it is no wonder that Indian members of the Legislative Council regarded the act as a threat to an orderly advance toward responsible government.

Another political decision of the Curzon regime that angered the nationalists was the reorganization in 1904 of the governing bodies of the Indian universities. The universities were largely self-governing through senates made up of representatives of the colleges, most of whom were Indian and many of whom were identified with the nationalist movement. The Universities Act, like the other measures, aimed at tightening British control and giving the government a larger share in management. Again this act was denounced by Indian leaders as a direct attack on the educated classes. The moderates were in despair, with their faith in British intentions increasingly undermined, much to the satisfaction of their extremist opponents.

The administrative action of Curzon's regime that had the most far-reaching effect, however, was undoubtedly the partition of Bengal into two provinces in 1905. For a number of years there had been complaints from officials that it was too large to be administered as a separate province. With a population of 78 million, it was larger than most countries, as it included what is now West Bengal, Bangladesh, Bihar and Orissa. The origin of the province was the *suba* of the Mughal empire which the East India Company had acquired in 1765 and to which other territories had been added as they were annexed in the early years of the nineteenth century. The reorganization, in which Bengal lost about eleven million of its population to the new province of East Bengal and Assam could be viewed, therefore, as a sensible administrative measure. The Indian nationalist leaders, however, saw it as a peculialry sinister action on the part of the British to weaken nationalism in general and Bengali nationalism in particular. Responding to the increasing frustration of even the moderate leaders as they failed to win concession from the British, as well as to the militant revolutionary fervor that was building up in Bengal and elsewhere, the agitation against petition by the leaders of the Indian National Congress helped to alter the temper and direction of the nationalist movement. Nowhere else in India was there such a close identification of geographic area and nationalist sentiment, and the partition seemed to be a rending of that motherland of which Bankim Chander Chatterji had sung in *Bande Mataram*. It was also a blow to the dominance of the Calcutta intelligentsia—the teachers, the lawyers, the journalists, the novelists and poets—who had made the city the intellectual capital, not just of the vast hinterland of Bengal, but of all India. And finally, although this was not always made explicit in the denunciations of the partition, the new East Bengal would have a Muslim majority, and many of the nationalists were Hindus who had their ancestral ties there. By this time there was a growing suspicion that the British administration were encouraging the Muslims to see the Indian National Congress with its nationalist ideology as a threat to the Muslims in community. From this point on, the argument that the British used the Muslims in a strategy of "Divide and Conquer" becomes an essential ingredient of that ideology. The reaction on the part of Muslim leaders to this Congress attack on the partition of Bengal was almost inevitable : they saw it as proof that the Congress was unwilling to give Muslims an opportunity for political control.

Curzon had a clear perception of the political consequences of partition: an inevitable clash between the imperial power and the nationalists. He had no doubt of the outcome or of its desirability. The government believed that the agitation against partition represented only the small Western-educated minority in Calcutta and argued, "it cannot be for the lasting good of any country that public opinion or what passes for it should be manufactured by a comparatively small number of people at a single center and should be disseminated thence for universal adoption."[3] The very strength of the opposition to the partition by the articulate Hindu upper classes underlined its value for some officials. It would restrict Nationalist areas of influence, while providing the Muslims with an opportunity to regain some of the status they had lost through Hindu economic and intellectual domination based in Calcutta. The Muslims, it was assumed, would reciprocate by showing a firm attachment to the government.

Partition put new vitality into the nationalists' cause by providing an opportunity for a defiant challenge to imperial power. There were many sources of this challenge, not all of which were coordinated, and some of which worked at cross-purposes. Numerous secret societies, which amalgamated religious devotion and nationalist fervor, had been formed in the last years of the nineteenth century. Most of them were in Bengal, but there were a number in Bombay where B.G. Tilak's influence was strong, and in Punjab, where the British suspected the eminent Indian National Congress leader, Lala Lajpat Rai, of being involved in terrorist activities.

New Radicalism

Indian nationalists were also stirred by the Japanese defeat of Russia in 1905. Now that a great Western power had been humiliated by a small Asian nation, Indians—and not just Bengali revolutionaries—began to wonder if India might not be able to repeat the Japanese experience and use force to defeat Great Britain. The dreams of the revolutionaries were also fed by the militant religious nationalism of Aurobindo Ghose and his followers, and for the

first time since 1857 the government was faced with political
assassinations and acts of sabotage. The secret societies responsible
for these activities probably never enrolled more than a few thousand members, most of whom were young students, but they provided a genuine alternative to the political gradualism of the Indian
National Congress.

An interesting aspect of the 1905 movement, and one that was
supported by many people who had no sympathy for the terrorists,
was a campaign to replace British goods of all kinds with those
manufactured in India. The emphasis on *swadeshi*, things belong-
ing to India, which was intended to strengthen the Indian economy
while at the same time hurting the British. indicates a concern to
give the nationalist movement a more indigenous base. The *swadeshi*
movement and the boycott were concrete manifestations of an
economic interpretation of modern Indian history that by this time
was widely accepted by nationalists. In barest outline, the argument was that the poverty of India had been caused by British rule.
Aside from the historical accuracy of this judgment, its value to a
nationalist movement is obvious: The poverty and economic back-
wardness of India were due not to anything inherent in Indian
society, but to the foreign intrusion. It was especially important to
the early nationalist leaders because they had so genuinely accepted
what may be called the nineteenth-century political interpretation
of Indian history: The British had saved India from anarchy and
chaos and given her peace and order. Thus it was no accident that
the most telling criticisms of the economic effect of British rule
came from Dadabhai Naoroji and R.C. Dutt, to both of whom, in
Dutt's phrase, "the Indian Empire was the grandest of human
institutions." Naoroji popularized the idea of "The Drain," the
idea that Indian wealth flowed to England in the form of high sala-
ries paid to the governing class and in the great excess of India's
exports over her imports. In the previous forty years £500 million
worth of goods had been drained to England, he estimated in 1901.
Here was the remedy for all of India's economic ills: Let her keep
what she produces; let her use her own raw materials, instead of
shipping them out of the country and then buying them back as
finished goods. Like Naoroji, Dutt backed the arguments in his
survey of nineteenth-century economic history with an impressive
array of statistics, coming to the conclusion that because of British
policies India was given "peace but not prosperity: . . . the manu-

facturers lost their industries; . . . the cultivators were ground down by a heavy and variable taxation; . . . the revenues were to a large extent diverted to England; and . . . recurring famines swept away millions of the population."[4]

The *swadeshi* movement in 1905 was thus an assertion of both spiritual and material independence, based on a reasoned, although perhaps fallacious, understanding of the working of economic forces. The extremists, contemptuous of the caution of the moderates, pressed for an unequivocal statement of support from the Indian National Congress for *swadeshi* and the idea of self-rule. The old liberal leadership compromised in 1906 by accepting a resolution that gave limited support to the boycott of British goods and the *swadeshi* ideals, but they insisted on reserving the right of interpretation of the meaning of the resolution. The Congress, Gokhale said, had "no aspirations except such as may be realized within the British Empire." This may have been true for the majority of the leadership, but the restless dynamism of the new nationalism spoke for the younger intelligentsia and the students, who by this time had become, in modern terms, politicized. "We have perceived one fact," Tilak declared, "that the whole of this administration, which is carried by a handful of Englishmen, is carried on with our assistance. . . . The point is to have the entire control in our hands."[5] A confrontation with imperial power was necessary, but this could be achieved through a boycott, without recourse to arms. Violence was not ruled out as a possible future weapon, but it was accepted that British power was too strong to be challenged. This belief in British invulnerability is a very important factor in explaining the quiescence of India.

The open clash between the moderates and the extremists came at the meeting of the Indian National Congress at Surat in 1907. The members of the New Party, as Tilak's followers were called, were ousted by the moderates, who demanded a pledge of loyalty to the old program of strictly constitutional action for reform of the existing administration. Tilak's followers did not form a separate organization as they still hoped to gain control of the Congress but Tilak's imprisonment on a charge of encouraging sedition deprived them of their most experienced leader. The price the Congress paid for the formal unity imposed by the moderates was, however, a loss of vitality.

At the same time the tensions that had generated the divisions in the Indian National Congress itself were having repercussions on Muslim leaders. The new radicalism, with its scarcely veiled appeal to violence as the most effective road to Indian freedom, and the quasi-religious vocabulary in which it expressed its aspirations, caused disquiet among Indian Muslims. Syed Ahmad Khan's forebodings that the nationalist movement pointed toward Hindu domination seemed confirmed, for an important element in the fierce antagonism aroused by the partition of Bengal was the charge by the Indian National Congress that the government had created a province in Eastern Bengal with a Muslim majority. The denunciation of the partition by the Congress, whose leadership was overwhelmingly Hindu, had been countered by Muslims in Eastern Bengal with expressions of support for the measure and in some areas by anti-Hindu riots. These outbreaks frequently had roots in the economic grievances of the peasants, but since the peasants were largely Muslim and the landlords were Hindus, the outbreaks easily assumed a religious character. Added to this sentiment of the economically disadvantaged was the dislike by members of the Muslim upper classes of Hindu political and social power. This latter group formed in 1906 the Muslim League, which challenged the claims of the Congress to speak for the nation by insisting that Muslims constituted a separate nationality.

Muslim League

The importance of the Bengal partition for Muslim sentiment has been bluntly stated by I.H. Qureshi, one of the most influential historians of modern Pakistan: "The Hindu attitude during the anti-partition agitation had convinced the Muslims of the futility of expecting any justice or fair play from the Hindu majority."[6] This harsh judgment has been challenged on the grounds that it is not based on sufficient evidence of Hindu behavior and that it ignores the government's policy of "divide and conquer," but these criticisms are irrelevant since Qureshi's statement reflects quite accurately how many Muslims appraised the situation. This anti-Hindu element was probably as essential for the development of Muslim nationalism in India as was the more positive expression of identity between religious and patriotic values within the Congress for Indian nationalism itself.

The founders of the Muslim League were not the Muslim counterparts of the founders of the Indian National Congress for they represented the landlords and the old Muslim ruling classes rather than the new professions created by the Western impact. As already stressed, this was a reflection of differences between Hindu and Islamic social organization. The Muslims who formed the League had prided themselves on staying out of politics, and their activity in 1906 was an indication that political activity could no longer be avoided. It was precisely this kind of political action that had been anathema to the older generation of Muslim leaders represented by Syed Ahmad Khan, who had envisaged ideal government in terms of rulers acting benevolently for the welfare of the people, not as a process of negotiating demands and applying pressures. The formation of the League indicated the conversion of the Muslim leaders to the new style of political life.

The objectives of the Muslim League as outlined in 1906 indicate the groping of the Muslim leaders for new policies for dealing with the government and the Hindu majority. Their desire "to promote among the Mussulmans of India feelings of loyalty to the British Government and to remove any misconceptions that may arise as to the intentions of Government" was a tacit recognition that both British suspicions of Muslims and Muslim dislike of British rule had to be eradicated. The protection and advance of the political rights and interests of Indian Muslims and their representation to the government expressed the conviction that Muslims must assert their special status. They were not a minority, but a nation. A final objective was "to prevent the rise among Mussulmans of India of any feelings of hostility towards other communities." A curious saving rider was attached to this: "without prejudice to other objects of the League."[7] The phrasing is ambiguous, but it probably recognizes that the assertion of Muslim rights might lead to Hindu-Muslim strife, and if so, the claiming of rights could not be forgone for the sake of communal harmony.

Constitutional Reforms

A conflict of interest was always latent in the Indian National Congress demand for representative institutions, and it became of central importance when the government announced the constitutional changes known as the Morley-Minto Reforms (after the governor general, Lord Minto, and the secretary of state for India, John Morley). These were embodied in the Government of India Act of 1909, one of the landmarks of Indian constitutional history.

The government denied that the constitutional changes were a response to nationalist agitation. Minto was still insisting as late as 1906 that nationalism in India was "altogether peculiar." In Europe national leaders had the support of the great majority of their fellow countrymen, but in India "there is no popular movement from below. The movement, such as it is, is impelled by the leaders of a class very small indeed in comparison to the population of India, who, if by some miracle they obtained the reins of Government, are totally incapable of ruling and would not for an instant be tolerated by the people of India as a whole."[8] Yet despite these protestations the aim of the reforms was to ensure that Indian cooperation which made the Indian administration possible. A number of the longstanding demands of the Indian National Congress were met, at least in a partial fashion, by the Government of India Act. The legislative councils were enlarged to permit increased Indian representation; an Indian was appointed to the governor general's Executive Council, and the members were allowed to discuss the budget. The principle of election was conceded by giving the franchise to certain groups and organizations—chambers of commerce, landowners, trade associations, local governments, and universities. This was far from a democratic suffrage, but Indian opinion regarded it as the first installment of representative government. The Congress, securely controlled by moderates, expressed its thanks in 1908 for the promise of "a large and liberal instalment of the reforms needed to give the people of this country a substantial share in the management of their affairs."[9]

The Government of India Act contained concessions acceptable not only to the moderate leaders of the Indian National Congress, but also to the rival Indian nationalism represented by the Muslim League. The objection by the Muslim leaders to any form of representative government was answered by provision of special constituencies for Muslims that guaranteed them places in the central and provincial legislative councils. The Muslim League welcomed the application of what they termed the principle of separate racial representation. The use of the word "racial" is interesting, for even if the League did not intend to suggest that Muslims constituted a separate "race" in India, at least it implies that something more than religious preferences separated them from the rest of the population. The full meaning of this position was not spelled out for many years, but logically it could only lead either to a binational state or to partition.

Although the moderate leaders who controlled the Indian National Congress had at first welcomed the reforms of 1909, they soon denounced the provision of special representation for Muslims as subversive of Indian nationhood. That no representation was guaranteed the Hindu miniorities in East Bengal, where the Muslims were in a majority, also rankled. Almost imperceptibly, the defense of Indian nationality was transformed in the discussions of 1910 into a defense of Hindu rights with regard to new Muslim privileges. The moderates, who had for so long refused to let any religious distinctions color their concept of India's nationhood, now found themselves driven to arguing in communal terms. As one speaker summed up this situation at the Congress meeting in 1910, it was not his intention to "say a word of discord. . . . At the same time . . . it will be sheer hypocrisy to deny the facts. . . . The Muhammedans have got an over-representation."[10] The proof adduced was that in the central Legislative Council there were thirteen Hindus and eleven Muslims, while the ratio in the general population was four Hindus to one Muslim.

The growing tension between Hindus and Muslims did not mean that all Muslims followed the leadership of the Muslim League. Sectarian conflicts within Islam itself were betrayed by the charge that the Muslim League was under control of Sunnis, the main branch of Muslims, who systematically excluded the members of the Shia sect. Others saw the special electorates working against the best interests of the Muslim masses, since the most conservative groups of Muslims were favored by the property franchise. Among those who in 1910 opposed any further extension of the principle was M.A. Jinnah, who later became the spokesman for the demand for a Muslim state in Pakistan. At the time, he believed that representative government could be established in India not based on religious communities. His change of mind reflected later developments in India's search for nationality, many of them the product of India's involvement in World War I, which had a decisive effect on India's national development.

Effect of World War I

In contrast to 1939, when there was such vociferous protest from nationalist leaders for India being taken into the war against Germany and other Axis powers without any consultation, there was little protest in 1914 or even discussion, as India's resources in manpower and materials were put at the disposal of the war effort. The change is partly an indication of a difference in evaluation of the international situation by the nationalist leaders. In 1914, most of them had accepted the British reading of the situation that India's international interests were identical with those of Britain, while in 1939 men like Jawaharlal Nehru, Subhas Chandra Bose, and Mahatma Gandhi had come to very different conclusions because of their ideological commitments. But the changes were also due to the fact that in 1939 India had become a far more independent and autonomous nation than it had been in 1914, with many of these changes related to the war itself. Some of these, such as the return of Gandhi to India and the emergence of India on the international scene will be noted in chapter 4 and 5, but it will be useful to mention others here, including the impact of the War on the Indian economy.

The economic effect of the First World War on India are hard to disentangle, since many changes might have taken place even without the cataclysm of the war. The general weakening of the economic and political position of Great Britain in relation to the other great powers would have made it difficult for Britain to have maintained its dominance of India. There were, however, changes that can be directly related to the War itself. An immediate impact was to make India more dependent on the British connection, for the growth of trade with other countries, which had been going on since the early years of the century was suddenly reversed. There was a drop of 43 per cent in exports and 34 percent in imports in the first year over prewar averages. This reflected both the loss of such markets as Germany, which had become India's best customer after the United Kingdom, and the diversion of shipping for war purposes. Added to this change in exports and imports was a new demand for supplies for India's own armies and those of Great Britain. The result was that prices rose very sharply for such necessities as salt, kerosene, and cotton cloth. Inflationary tendencies increased because of speculation and hoarding. Military demands on the railways intensified the distribution problems for these commodities. And while prices of manufactured and imported goods increased, the prices paid for agricultural products went down because of good harvests, which meant that the peasants were hard hit by the rising costs. The cheap food did not help the townspeople either, because of the dislocation of the transportation system. The discontents and suffering occasioned by these economic problems were felt everywhere in India, leading to the first peasant movements under Indian National Congress sponsorship and a series of strikes in 1917 in the great cities. Perhaps more than any other single factor, the economic dislocation caused by the war explains the new openness of the masses to the political agitation initiated by the Congress under the leadership of Gandhi.

Yet at the same time that the economic conditions of the masses were worsening, there was a marked expansion in industrial productivity occasioned by the new military demands and the decrease in imports. The first important steel manuacturing company was established by the Tata family in 1903. The Tatas raised their capital from Indian sources, although they made use of American and European technicians. The achievement of large-scale production virtually coincided with the outbreak of the war and the Tatas were able to supply large amounts of the steel formerly imported from Great Britain. Other industries, notably textiles and light engineering works, also expanded in response to military needs. The production of munitions and war materials of all kinds was encouraged by the establishment of the Munitions Board in 1917. All of these new industries were severely hit by the loss of military markets when the war ended, but they gave an impetus to industrial development that was never lost.

The expansion of the Indian army was one of the most remarkable wartime phenomena, and it had important psychological and political repercussions. At the beginning of the war the army had consisted of about 230,000 Indians and 80,000 British officers and men, but before the end of hostilities over a million men were recruited. This was done without conscription, but local landlords in the great recruiting grounds of Punjab and the United Provinces applied pressure in the villages, while increases in pay made army service attractive to the peasants. Hundreds of thousands of these troops served overseas and throughout the Indian borderlands, breaking or disrupting the old ties that bound them to their villages and regions. The recruitment of Indians as soldiers in such large number and their use throughout the major theaters of war also reinforced the demand that had long been made by the Indian nationatists for the granting of officers' commissions to Indians. A tentative beginning was made in 1917 when Indians became eligible for commissions as lieutenants. The nationalist interest in the rights of Indians to receive military promotions was important in fostering a sense of respect for Indian soldiers as defenders of the nation, and not just as the mercenaries of the foreign conqueror.

Revival of Nationalist Activity

The ferment engendered throughout India by the war restored the vigor that nationalist politics had lost after the divisions created at Surat in 1907. Factions often worked at cross-purposes, and the old splits between the moderates and the extremists and between the Hindus and the Muslims were not healed, but out of their interaction came a vitality that gave a new direction to Indian nationalism. For some groups the war offered an opportunity to attack the British while they were distracted in Europe. The revolutionary bodies in Bengal and the Punjab continued their policy of political assassination and sabotage. Indian revolutionaries in exile, notably those in the Ghadr party in the United States, gave them financial help and smuggled arms to them. The exiles received some help from the Germans, but their organization was inefficient, the British watchful, and the Germans unconcerned with India. Their subversive campaign was never really damaging. The terrorists' major accomplishment was to keep local officials off balance and make them aware of the strength of the opposition to British rule in India. The old argument that only a handful of malcontents were concerned with nationalist aspirations began to disappear from official reports, to be replaced by what is perhaps an exaggerated fear of violence and of the power of public opinion. The revolutionaries also supplied martyrs to Indian nationalism, for some of the terrorists were put to death.

The revival of the Indian National Congress as an active political force during the war years owed much to B.G. Tilak, who had been released from prison in 1914, and to a new personality in Indian nationalist life, Mrs. Annie Besant. Mrs. Besant has often been a subject of ridicule in the West, but her contribution to the Indian nationalist movement was serious and long lasting. She had gone to India in 1893 to work for the Theosophical Society, and as an outstanding orator and a writer with a gift for clear, dramatic expression, she had made theosophy a potent force in Indian intellectual life, especially in south India. Theosophy is a complex mixture of mystical symbols and doctrines but her emphasis on the superiority of Hindu ethical and theological concepts won her a hearing among the educated classes. Although by temperament and political conviction a moderate believing in constitutional gradualism, she allied herself with Tilak in a political campaign that demanded home rule for India. Her hope was that Tilak might be taken back into the Congress, which, revitalized by his energy, could then pressure the government through popular agitation into further constitutional reforms.

Tilak confined his activities to the Marathi-speaking regions of Bombay, while Mrs. Besant used the network of Theosophical Societies already in existence to organize the most extensive propaganda compaign that had yet been attempted in India. The program of the Home Rule League was "Home Rule for India," but there was no demand for British withdrawal. Tilak was too cautious to make such a public statement, and Mrs. Besant hoped for cooperation and friendship between the British and the Indians. The success of the Home Rule League in stirring up popular opinion forced the moderate leaders of the Indian National Congress to cooperate with Tilak, and by 1916 he once more had an important voice in its decisions. His old liberal opponent Gokhale had died in 1915, leaving Tilak a position of undisputed influence in Bombay. At the same time that the factions within the Congress were reuniting, Mrs. Besant and Tilak were working for a rapprochement with the Muslim League.

Such a rapprochement was possible in 1916 because of the changes that Muslim sentiment had undergone in India since the founding of the Muslim League in 1906. Then the emphasis had been on loyalty to the British regime and a dislike of representative government based on a fear of the Hindu dominance. This fear did not disappear after 1906, but it was put in a new perspective by changes in the Islamic world. First of all the nationalist revival in Turkey under the Young Turks in 1908 caught the imagination of many Muslim intellectuals in India. Then when war broke

out between Italy and Turkey in 1911, echoes of the ancient antagonism between Islam and Christendom were awakened. A senti-
mental attachment developed in India toward Turkey as the chief
Islamic state, and toward the Turkish sultan as the caliph, of the
Muslim world community. The entry of Turkey into the war on
the side of Germany made her Britain's enemy, thus confirming
the anti-British prejudices which were deeper and stronger in many
Muslims than the alliances with the British forged by Syed Ahmad
Khan and his successors. The new anti-British sentiment found
an outlet in a number of newspapers, many of them in Urdu. The
most forceful figure in this new movement was Abul Kalam Azad
(1888-1958), who became the spokesman for "nationalist Muslims"; that is, those who believed that all Indians should join in a
common front in the Indian National Congress against British
rule.

The outcome of these activities was one of the landmarks in
the development of Indian nationalism : the joint meeting of the
Indian National Congress and the Muslim League in Lucknow in
1916. The two parties worked out a scheme of constitutional
reform, with the overall aim of raising India to equal status with
the other self-governing dominions of the British Empire. The
first step was to be the proclamation by the king-emperor that self-
government would be conferred on India at an early date. Major
compromises were made by both organizations, with the Congress
accepting the principle of separate repressntation for Muslims and
the League agreeing to the principle of representative government.
The Muslims were promised more than their proportional number
of seats, but they would not have a majority in any province, not
even in Bengal where they were 52 percent of the population, nor
could they ever hope to achieve one, since they specifically agreed
not to stand in any of the general constituencies. There was a
strong emphasis on provincial autonomy and on the full representation of Indians in the army and the Civil Service.

The home rule agitation and the Congress-League Pact at
Lucknow demonstrated that there was now widespread support for
nationalist aspirations from all segments of the population and
that further delay would only weaken the moderate elements. The
result was the announcement in Parliament on August 20, 1917,
that the policy of the British government and the government of
India was "the increasing association of Indians in every branch of

the administration and the gradual development of self-governing
institutions with a view to the progressive realization of responsible
government in India as an integral part of the British Empire."
The secretary of state for India referred to this statement as "the
most momentous utterance ever made in India's chequered history,"[11] but as far as Indian opinion was concerned, it was only a
formal recognition of what had long been taken for granted.

The 1917 announcement promised "responsible government,"
not "self-government." The distinction was important, since it
made clear that the imperial power would still exercise ultimate
control, including deciding when India was ready for further ad-
vances. But the rulers would no longer be mere bureaucrats.
They would become responsive to an electorate and share power
with popularly elected ministers. Edwin Montagu, the secretary
of state for India, told the civil servants and officials what
this meant : "They must learn to be politicians".[12] The transition
was not easy for a class that had prided itself on giving the Indian
people what was good for them, not what they wanted, making it
a point of honor never to explain or argue. It was not strange,
as Montagu pointed but, that the strongest opposition to his proposals came, not from the Conservatives in England, but from the
bureaucracy in India.

The implications of the 1917 announcement were spelled out
in what is known as the Montagu-Chelmsford Reforms, after
Montagu and Lord Chemsford, then governor general. The most
striking feature was the introduction at the provincial level of the
principle of dyarchy, or divided responsibility. All the branches of
the provincial administration were divided, with some under the
direct control of the governor, who would continue to be a British
appointee, and some under the control of ministers responsible to
the elected legislatures. Among the "reserved" subjects were finance,
police, and the administration of justice; the "transferred" subjects
included education, public health, public works, and agriculture.
The legislative councils were greatly enlarged, and although the
governors still nominated some members, the majority were to be
elected.

This last provision raised the thorniest problem of constitutional reform: the nature of the franchise. The Montagu-Chelmsford Reforms recognized that communal electorates perpetuated
and deepened class divisions, teaching men to think in terms of

partisan groups rather than of the nation, and that to give a minority representation because it was weak was a positive encouragement for it to stay weak so that it would not lose privileges. Yet no alternative seemed possible that would be satisfactory to the Muslims, especially after the concessions of the Morley-Minto Reforms of 1909 and the Congress-League Pact of 1916. In the end, special representation was given not only to Muslims but also to numerous other groups : Indian Christians, Sikhs, Anglo-Indians, Europeans landlords, universities, chambers of commerce. Hindus did not receive separate electorates, but they voted in the general constituencies, where it was assumed they would be in the majority. The right to vote was based on property qualification as well as race and religion, and it differed from province to province depending upon the strength of minority groups. The qualifications were also different for the central Legislative Council. Appoximately 5.5 million persons received the vote and, since women were excluded, this meant about 7 percent of the adult male population.

*   *   *

The 1919 Constitution was, in many ways, a generous and forward-looking document, but yet it did not concede that India was a nation. Instead, it spoke of India as "a sisterhood of states," presided over by a central government dealing with matters of common concern.[13] In 1885 this might have been a promise that would have caught the imagination of the nationalist leaders; by 1919 it was outdated.

NOTES

[1]Quoted in S. Gopal, *British Policy in India 1858-1905* (Cambridge : Cambridge University Press, 1965), p. 298.

[2]Speech by D.F. MacKenzie, August 7, 1899, in *Proceedings of the Council of the Lieut.-Governor of Bengal* 1899, Vol. 31.

[3]Great Britain, *Parliamentary Papers*, 1905, Vol. 71, Cd. 2746 p. 17

[4]R.C. Dutt, *The Economic History of India in the Victorian Age* (London: Kegan Paul, 1950), pp. xviii-xix.

[5]Quoted in Wolpert, *Tilak and Gokhale*, pp. 196-197.

[6]Qureshi, *The Struggle for Pakistan*, pp. 29-30.

[7]Muslim Resolution at Dacca, December 30, 1906, in C.H. Philips, *et al* (eds,), *The Evolution of India and Pakistan, 1858-1947* (London : Oxford University Press, 1962), p. 194.

[8]Minto to Morley, November 4, in *ibid.*, p. 76.

[9]Resolutions of the Twenty-Fourth National Congress, 1908 in *The Indian National Congress.*

[10]H. Vishandas, in *Report of the Twenty-Fifth National Congress,* 1910 (Allahabad : Indian Press, 1911), p. 89.

[11]Great Britain, *Parliamentary Papers,* 1918, Vol. 8, Cd. 9109, "Report on Indian Constitutional Reforms".

[12]Edwin Montagu, *An Indian Diary* (London : Heinemann, 1930), p. 216.

[13]Great Britain, *Parliamentary Papers,* 1918, Vol. 8, "Indian Constitution Reforms," p. 277.

4

The
Emergence of
Gandhi

Before the Constitutional Reforms of 1919 were drafted, a preliminary report noted that the granting of voting rights in India was only a partial step toward public participation in government. "We have to bring about", the report noted, "the most radical revolution in the people's traditional ideas of the relation between ruler and ruled, and it will be a difficult and even dangerous business, for it is neither safe nor easy to meddle with traditional ideas in India."[1]

The task of transforming the attitudes of the Indian masses toward their rulers was undertaken quite self-consciously by Mohandas Karamchand Gandhi (1869-1948). His successes and failures constitute in large measure both his own political biography and that of the Indian nationalist movement.

Gandhi was not the father of the Indian nation, as he has often been called, for the essential groundwork had been laid by the time he made his initial impact on Indian life. His peculiar genius was his understanding that the existing Indian social structure, with the enormous importance of its religions symbols, could be made part of the new political process. His great success was in giving millions of people for the first time a sense of involvement in the nation's destiny. More than any other leader Gandhi helped to create the psychological climate that is a prerequisite of nationalism, in which individual identity is dependent upon national identity. But this extraordinary achievement, which was perhaps unmatched by any other leader in modern times in the magnitude of the numbers involved, carried with it the fulfillment of the demands of the competing Muslim nationalism. The tensions created by Gandhi's leadership, dynamic and necessary though they were for Indian nationalist experience, completed the Muslim nationalist awakening that had begun in the late nineteenth century.

Gandhi's active involvement in the Indian political scene dates only from 1919, but by then he was already one of the best-known Indians of his generation, respected alike by the Indians and the British. He had won his reputation in South Africa, where he had worked for twenty years on behalf of the Indian community in their struggle against the discriminatory laws and practices of the South African government. Although he abandoned a successful law practice to live a life of poverty in the commune that he founded on the basis of Tolstoy's Christian primitivism, he remained attached to the law courts. His skilled mind was able to operate within the framework of British jurisprudence to gain redress from injustices. His devotion to nonviolence in South Africa, as later in India, was directed by the strain in the Indian religious tradition that believes violence leads to the enslavement of the soul. He was also influenced by the emphasis in the radical Christian pacifist tradition of repaying evil with good, of turning the other cheek, and of expressing the divine will through an acceptance of suffering. Such ideas became the rationale for his "experiments with truth", attempts to live what he considered a wholly natural life. Many of these experiments were concerned with areas that seemed to others irrelevant to political life, such as diet and sexual continence. But the one direct political consequence was what he called the technique of *satyagraha,* or nonviolent action. Especially when the weak confronted their oppressors, this was the ideal weapon, with the aim not conquest, but a change of heart leading the strong to seek reconciliation with those they had wronged. Such ideas were remote from the political philosophy of the Indian moderate leaders, but men like Gokhale, who introduced Gandhi to the Indian political world, saw that behind those ideas was the same assumption that guided their own activity—that if the possessors of power could be brought to see the justice of the demands made upon them, they would yield.

During the war years, although Gandhi was in India, he held aloof from politics. To Edward Montagu, the secretary of state, he seemed to be, in contrast to some of the other Indian leaders, "a social reformer with a real desire to find grievances and to cure them, not for any reasons of self-advertisement, but to improve the conditions of his fellow man."[2] But there was another side to Gandhi's noninvolvement in nationalist politics during the war years. He was a leader, not a follower. "You have every right to kick me out, to demand my head, or to punish me whenever and howsoever you choose", he once told his followers, "but as long as you chose to keep me as your leader you must accept my conditions, you must accept my dictatorship."[3] Such an understanding of leadership would be difficult to enforce in a nationalist movement still dominated by the great figures of the past—Tilak, Gokhale, S.N. Banerjee, Lajpat Rai, C.R. Das, and Mrs. Besant. Neither his methods nor his understanding of the Indian situation marched with theirs, whether they were moderates like Banerjee or radicals like Tilak. His only recourse was to stand on the sidelines of the national movement, but he did not wait idly. As part of the preparation for the deeper involvement that he expected, he turned his attention in a direction that, as commonplace as it may now seem, was then novel : He began an investigation of the grievances of the peasants and workers.

Because of his record of dealing with the problem of indentured laborers in South Africa, Gandhi was urged in 1917 to go to Champaran in Bihar to see what could be done to help the peasants who were in debt to the indigo planters. Since indigo planters, many of whom were European, were notorious for their ill-treatment of the peasants who worked for them, Gandhi's appearance as the champion of the peasants aroused great interest, although the negotiations were inconclusive. The effect of his presence as reported by a British official in the area was a foreshadowing of the next thirty years.

We may look on Mr. Gandhi as an idealist, a fanatic, or a revolutionary according to our particular opinions, but to the *raiyats* he is their liberator, and they credit him with extraordinary powers. He moves about their villages asking them to lay their grievances before him, and he is transfiguring the imaginations of masses of ignorant men with visions of an early millenium.[4]

One side of Gandhi's genius was his appeal as a charismatic leader to people in whom the vocabulary of the old nationalist politics had awakened no response. The other was his ability as a negotiator with the planters and government officials to obtain a modest redress of the peasants' grievances. The same techniques were demonstrated later in the year when serious labor troubles developed in the great textile mills in Ahmedabad, near Gandhi's home. The chief British official in the area asked him to make peace between the millowners and the workers; but when the owners refused to accept arbitration, Gandhi advised the workers to go on strike. He lacked the funds to support the strikers, and when they began to waver he went on a fast, not to intimidate the millowners, he insisted, but to purify the workers so they would have the courage to endure suffering and starvation. The result was that the employers agreed to arbitration, and the workers accepted less than they had originally demanded.

Reactions to the Rowlatt Acts

Gandhi's influence at Champaran and Ahmedabad provided him with a base for political operations and opened up new possibilities for channeling the resentment against British rule and the desire for participation in public life into new forms of political action. By 1919 he was ready to use his power in the service of Indian nationhood.

Although the formal center of political concern continued to be the deliberations of the Indian National Congress on the new constitution, three specific issues usurped public interest after 1918: the Rowlatt Acts, the Amritsar massacre, and the Khilafat agitation. It was these issues, not the broader question of constitutional change, that provided Gandhi with his platform for entrance into Indian politics.

The Rowlatt Acts permitted the imprisonment without trial of persons suspected of subversion. Even before the acts were passed they had aroused violent opposition in all sections of the Indian political world. This reaction was a reflection of the curious relationship that still existed between the Indian nationalists and the

British, based on the presumption that the governing power was committed to the extension and protection of the political freedoms guaranteed by British law and jurisprudence. Gandhi's own commitment to action within the legal framework was shaken, for, as he put it, the government itself had moved outside this framework by passing laws that were "unjust, subversive of the principles of liberty and justice, and destructive of the elementary rights of individuals on which the safety of the community as a whole and the state itself is based."[5] His remedy was to call for a one-day *hartal*, or general strike, on April 6.

Despite Gandhi's emphasis on the peaceful nature of *hartal*, there were many outbreaks of violence as mobs clashed with the police. The situation was already very tense in the Punjab, and when Gandhi attempted to enter the province, he was arrested and sent back to Bombay. The arrest of other popular leaders led to further violence, and the civil authorities, convinced that they could no longer maintain order, called in the military. All processions and demonstrations were forbidden, especially in the city of Amritsar, where a number of Europeans had been murdered by a mob after the police had fired on a procession. In disregard of the order of General Reginald Dyer, the officer commanding the troops in the area, a meeting was called in protest on April 13. Thousands of people had gathered in Jallianwala Bagh, an enclosed square in a congested part of the city, when Dyer arrived with 150 soldiers — one hundred were Indian. He stationed them at the only exist from the enclosure and gave the order to fire. A British journalist who was present described Dyer's action:

> Without a word of warning, he opened fire at about a hundred yards range upon a dense crowd. . . . The panic stricken multitude broke at once, but for ten consecutive minutes he kept up a merciless fusillade . . . on that seething mass of humanity, caught like rats in a trap, vainly rushing for the few narrow exits or lying flat on the ground to escape the rain of bullets, which he personally directed at the points where the crowd was the thickest. The "targets", to use his own words, were good. . . . He had killed, according to the official figures wrung out of the government months later, 379, and he left about 200 wounded on the ground, for whom, again

to use his own words, he did not consider it his "job" to take the slightest thought.[6]

Nothing of this kind had happened in living memory in India, and Indian political leaders of all persuasions denounced the Amritsar massacre as a betrayal of the British promises for constitutional reform. They did not all agree, however, that the time had come to end attempts at cooperation. Rabindranath Tagore, who had received the Nobel Prize for his poetry, showed his disapproval of Amritsar by renouncing the knighthood the British had given him; but he feared that the violence of the mob would be equally destructive of the values and decencies of life. At the very beginning of the twentieth century he had expressed his foreboding : "The naked passion of self-love of Nations, in its drunken delirium of greed, is dancing to the clash of steel and the howling verses of vengeance."[7] It now seemed that India would be caught up in the same demonic force of nationalism that was destroying the West. The Gandhian movement, by appealing to the masses even though it used the language of nonviolence, seemed to Tagore to threaten to let loose in India the same floods of unreason. He warned Gandhi that the violence that had followed the first *hartal* had shown that "power in all its forms is irrational. . . Passive resistance is a force which is not necessarily moral in itself; it can be used against truth as well as for it."[8]

Gandhi had come to somewhat the same conclusion as he heard of outbreaks of violence that were occurring throughout the country, and he called for an end of the strike. He had made, he said, a "Himalayan miscalculation', in starting a *satyagraha* movement before the people were educated : "Before one can be fit for the practice of civil disobedience one must have rendered a willing and respectful obedience to the slate laws. . . . It is only when a person has thus obeyed the laws of society scrupulously that he is in a position to judge as to which particular rules are good and just and which unjust and iniquitous."[9]

It was a sense of timing, then, not a change of heart about the rightness of his methods, that led Gandhi to urge the end of the first tentative non-violent protests in the spring of 1919. The decision that the people were not yet ready for a confrontation with the British and that the old methods of cooperation would have to continue was strengthened by the government's appointment of the Hunter Commission to inquire into the Amritsar massacre, which Gandhi expected to condemn the actions of General Dyer and the political authorities. Even if they were not condemned, awaiting the outcome of the commission's deliberations would give him more time to continue the education program for an effective non-violent movement. When the Indian National Congress held its annual session at Amritsar in December 1919, he led the fight for a decision to cooperate with the government by helping to work out the new constitution. This was a direct challenge to the old extremists and their supporters who favored refusing any further compromises. Tilak, attending his last session of the Congress, argued for denunciation of the constitution as "inadequate, unsatisfactory and disappointing" ; but Gandhi carried the day, and the resolution approving cooperation was passed.

Khilafat Movement

Within a year Gandhi was to make what seemed a complete about-face : He led the Indian National Congress into the non-cooperation movement, rejecting all the forms of participation in the constitutional framework he had persuaded the nationalists to accept in December 1919. The report of the Hunter Commission and the growing unrest among Muslims associated with the Khilafat movement were the immediate determinants of this new direction in Gandhi's leadership.

Commenting on the report of the Hunter Commission on the Amritsar massacre, Sarojini Naidu, one of the ablest of the many women who became leaders of the nationalist movement, remarked, "Our friends revealed their ignorance; our enemies their insolence."[10] Although the Hunter Commission concluded that the military measures were unduly harsh, the report stressed the provocation of the mob. The report shook Gandhi's remaining faith in British good intentions and released him from his pledge of cooperation.

The Khilafat movement arose out of the victorious Allies' treatment of Turkey, which had supported the Germans and shared in their defeat. General sympathy for the suffering of a Muslim country was sharpened by the position of the Turkish sultan as caliph (or khalif), the chief dignitary of the Islamic world. The caliph had not been of great importance to Indian Muslims previously, except for the *ulama*, or Islamic theologians, who had always been inclined towards an anti-British position. The Khilafat movement, which was organized in India to protest the division of the Ottoman Empire and the consequent weakening of the authority of the caliph, did not have any very clearly defined aims. It was essentially an emotional reaction to a humiliation of Islam by the Western—and Christian—nations.

Gandhi saw in the anti-British sentiment engendered by the Khilafat movement the possibility of a rapprochement with the Islamic community in 1919. Accepting the presidency of the Khilafat committee, formed to protest the dismemberment of Turkey, Gandhi worked closely with the leaders of the movement in India, with the result that the committee agreed to his proposal to initiate a program of non-cooperation. Gandhi's Hindu collea-gues had misgivings over this decision, but Gandhi saw it as the great breakthrough in the cause both of Muslim-Hindu unity and of a national acceptance of the method of *satyagraha* as a way of gaining freedom. To those who reminded him of the violence, in-cluding the dreadful events at Amritsar, that had followed the first experiments in *satyagraha* in April 1919, Gandhi replied that no country has ever risen without being purified through the fire of suffering and that India could not escape from slavery without paying the costs of self-purification.

Non-Cooperation Movement

Gandhi's task was now to convince the Indian National Con-gress to adopt a policy of nonviolence and noncooperation. Excite-ment mounted as Gandhi's appeals for Hindu-Muslim unity and the acceptance of the program of noncooperation spread through-out the country. A special session of the Congress convened in September 1920 in Calcutta and accepted Gandhi's proposals. The government's treatment of the Muslims and the condoning of the Amritsar massacre left the people of India no alternative, according to the resolution, but to adopt "the policy of progressive non-violent noncooperation, until the said wrongs are righted and *swaraj* is established."[11]

There was no definition of *swaraj*, and the vagueness was deliberate. For the educated classes, who were deeply committed to Western political institutions, it meant democratic, parliamen-

tary government on the British model ; for Gandhi it had an
almost apolitical meaning. "Abandonment of the fear of death"
or "the ability to regard every inhabitant of India as our own
brother or sister"[12] were some of the definitions he used in an attempt to give content to the term; but fundamentally it encompas-
ed a style of living and an attitude summed up in his own life.
This meant the renunciation of much from the modern Western
world—including industrialism and technology—that the older
generation of nationalist leaders, moderate or extremist, had regarded as essential for the future well-being of India. That noncooperation struck at the heart of the old collaboration was made
clear in his enumeration of the steps that were to be followed :

1. surrender of titles and all honorary offices under the
    government
2. withdrawal of children from schools and colleges
3. boycott by lawyers and litigants of law courts
4. refusal of candidates to stand for election in the new
    legislative councils and of voters to vote
5. boycott of foreign goods

The resolution concluded with a strong plea for the revival of
hand-spinning and hand-weaving in every home, partly as an economic measure, but more importantly so that "an opportunity
should be given in the first stage of non-cooperation to every man,
woman and child for . . . discipline and self-sacrifice."[13]
None of the measures that Gandhi proposed were wholly new
—the Bengal extremists had organized effective boycotts of British
goods in 1905—but taken all together, and including such momentous political steps as the refusal to take part in the elections to
the new councils, the Congress was being asked to make fundamental decisions about Indian nationhood. The emphasis was no
longer on hurting the British or even on making India strong
through home industries; the demand was for a radical reorienta-
tion of national life. Rabindranath Tagore, speaking for the
intellectual elite, sensed that the anti-intellectual and anti-rational
elements might combine with the emphasis on the Indian past to
frustrate the growth of community based on reason and mutual
understanding. "Our present struggle to alienate our heart and
mind from the West," he wrote, "is an attempt at spiritual

suicide."[14]   He was impatient with the emphasis on spinning in the
new program. *Swaraj*, he argued, "cannot be established on cheap
clothing ; its foundation is in the mind."[15] Tagore, who first called
Gandhi "Mahatma," now saw a special danger in the willingness
of the people to accept Gandhi's words as truth without any kind
of verification.

> Those for whom authority is needed in place of reason will
> invariably accept despotism in place of freedom. . . . We have
> had enough magic in this country, magical revelation, magical
> healing, and all kinds of divine intervention in mundane
> affairs. . . . Where Mahatma Gandhi has declared war against
> the tyranny of the machine which is oppressing the whole
> world, we are all enroled under his banner. But we must refuse
> to accept as our ally the illusion-haunted, magic-ridden, slave-
> mentality that is at the root of all the poverty and insult under
> which our country groans.[16]

The Gandhian message was thus for many in 1920 a call to
leave that search for accommodation with the modern world,
which had been the hallmark of the nationalist movement, and to
replace it with an inward-looking vision of traditional Indian
society, purified and cleansed, but nevertheless premodern and
preindustrial.   This could only end in suffering and loss for the
participants, most of whom had careers based on the educational
and legal institutions they were being called upon to boycott. And
while they were being asked to give up the opportunities of exer-
cising power through participating in new legislative councils, they
were being told at the same time that they must renounce the use
of violence, the alternative method that had been used with telling
effect against the British in the early years of the century.

In personal terms the acceptance of noncooperation meant
that power in the nationalist movement would pass from those
who now controlled it—C. R. Das, Motilal Nehru, Annie Besant,
M.M. Malaviya, Lala Lajpat Rai, M.A. Jinnah—to Gandhi and
his followers. Most of the old leaders, with the exception of
Jinnah, were to make some kind of accommodation with Gandhi,
but power is never easily given up. This was particularly true
when they felt that they stood for the modern world over against
Gandhi's traditionalism.

Complicating this division was the seeming contradiction of the very considerable support Gandhi received from the great industrialists of Western India, notably the cotton manufacturers. A cynical explanation is that they saw in Gandhi a power that could free them from the competition of European industries, but another factor may be equally important and not really out of keeping with the first. The industrialists of Western India were drawn, on the whole, from the traditional trading classes and were far less committed to the values of the modern world, less alienated from the Indian tradition, than the educated elite of Calcutta and its environs. Gandhi appealed to this sense of tradition and helped them to fulfill their classic role as men of affairs who recognized saintliness and paid for its upkeep but did not feel compelled to emulate it. But they were modern men, too, in many ways more so than the lawyers, journalists, and teachers who had shaped the early phases of nationalism. The anti-intellectualism of the Gandhian movement of which Tagore complained was not just the obscurantism of the rural past. It was also an expression of the values of business and commercial classes which were becoming a potent force in Indian political life. The old nationalist movement had drawn both its leadership and its support from a relatively small segment of society, and the success of the Gandhian movement in reaching out to new groups inevitably made for tension.

Non-Cooperation Begins

When the Indian National Congress met for its regular session at Nagpur at the end of December 1920, Gandhi was in a position to win assent for his revolutionary program, even from some of those who had opposed him at Calcutta. He won overwhelming approval for the noncooperation resolution, but he also showed his knowledge of the needs of a modern political party by preparing a new constitution that revolutionized the working of the Congress as a political organization. Village cells were made the basic unit of the Congress, and arrangements were made to set them up throughout the country. These were then grouped into districts and provincial committees, with election to the larger unit coming from below. At the top was the All-India Congress Committee with the executive power in the hands of the small Working Commttttee. Since anyone who paid four annas a year, (about ten cents) could be a member of the Indian National Congress, its membership was drawn from a wide spectrum of society, and the system of committees made for a democratic structure. The whole organization, however, could be tightly controlled by the Working Committee. The Congress also became a continuously functioning organization, and the executive could make its power felt throughout the country. At Nagpur, Gandhi's critics began to see that, while he might use the vocabulary of religious sentiment, he was also a superb political tactician.

Even in the perspective of history it is hard to say whether the first noncooperation program was a success or a failure. Elections were held; the legislative councils conducted their business; the schools and colleges were not emptied; foreign goods continued to be bought and sold; and in the end the program was formally revoked. But if, as Gandhi himself would have insisted, results are measured in terms of means, not ends, then the noncooperation program during 1921 brought about changes both in the quality of Indian nationalism and in the response of the administration to it. The watershed of 1921 ended for many the long dream of collaboration with the British.

Of even greater significance, the 1921 movement awakened a response throughout India. The masses had often been stirred before, for nothing is more false to the realities of Indian society than to picture it as apathetic and unmoved; its susceptibility to passionate involvement is attested by a multitude of religious movements and sectarian groups. But in 1921 this capacity for passion—and, Gandhi argued, for suffering—was harnessed for the first time to the aims of a nationalist organization. A high administrative official summed up the situation late in 1921 by saying that Gandhi "is now regarded not only as a great national hero, but, by the ignorant, as semi-divine."[17] What he missed was of crucial importance: If Gandhi was regarded as semi-divine, it was because he was a great national hero, and not the other way about. Divinities are a commonplace in India, and in themselves are not likely to impress the masses, who may be ignorant but are generally shrewd. The quality that in India defines divinity is power, and Gandhi now possessed power.

The noncooperation movement that began in January 1921 was not a civil disobedience campaign. That was to come later. The first stage required the education of the masses in the true

meaning of *swaraj,* gaining recruits for propaganda and organizational work, inspiring faith in the resolutions passed by the Congress, and, always a matter of the greatest concern for Gandhi,
raising money to support the movement. Gandhi and his followers
moved about the country making speeches, holding meetings with
key provincial leaders, and filling the columns of the movement's
newspaper, *Young India,* with discussions of the meaning of noncooperation. Jawaharlal Nehru has left an account of what the
movement meant, especially to the young intellectuals.

> Many of us who worked for the Congress programme lived in
> a kind of intoxication during the year 1921. We were full of
> excitement and optimism and a buoyant enthusiasm. . . . We
> worked hard, harder than we had ever done before, for we
> knew that the conflict with the Government would come
> soon. . . . We had a sense of freedom and a pride in that free-
> dom. The old feeling of oppression and frustration was com-
> pletely gone. There was no more whispering, no roundabout
> legal phraseology to avoid getting into trouble with the autho-
> rities. We said what we felt and shouted it from the house
> tops.[18]

This sense of excitement, of possibilities opening up for India,
led many individuals to perform dramatic acts of self-sacrifice in
the service of the nationalist cause. Thousands of students left the
government colleges and joined the new National Colleges set up
by the Congress. A number of distinguished lawyers, including
Vallabhbhai Patel, Rajendra Prasad, Rajagopalachari, all of whom
were later to hold high positions in the first government of independent India after 1947, gave up their practices. The spinning of
thread and the wearing of homespun cloth, *khadi* was an integral
part of the program. "Love of foreign cloth," Gandhi preached,
"brought foreign domination, pauperism and what is worse, shame
to many a home."[19] The simple white "Gandhi cap" became a
symbol of support for the national cause. In a country of extraordinary diversity of dress and manners, the adoption of such an
easily recognizable symbol was a stroke of genius, the one thing
that high caste and low, rich and poor, the Punjabi, the Madrasi,
the Bengali, could use without much difficulty. In the same way
the spinning of thread might not do much to alter economic condi-

tions, but the experience of working together in great mass meetings gave people an exhilarating sense of participation in the political process, as did another common feature of the movement, the burning of foreign cloth. People would collect the cloth and then gather for a great bonfire. Gandhi's defense of this practice, which seemed to many so wasteful in a land where people went naked because they could not afford clothing, exhibited the blend of passionate religious imagery and practical common sense that was at once appealing and confusing. To wear foreign clothing was sinful, he argued, because it deprived the Indian weaver of the right to work. "I must consign my foreign garments to the flames and thus purify myself. . . . I must refuse to insult the naked by giving them clothes they do not need, instead of giving them work which they sorely need."[20]

The involvement of women in the political struggle, a new element in the nationalist movement, was closely related to the emphasis on spinning and the regeneration of the country's economic life. Telling them that the economic and moral salvation of India rested with them, Gandhi appealed to the women to set an example of self-denial, asking them to give up the use of foreign goods for both themselves and their children. A woman must, "refuse to adorn herself for men, including her husband, if she will be an equal partner with man." Traditional Indian society emphasized the necessity of the good woman submitting herself to her husband's wishes, while at the same time it exalted her role as mother and giver of life. Gandhi's message that women could achieve an equality with men, or even in fact a kind of superiority through methods based upon the most time-honored concepts of wifely duty, must have had a profound psychological appeal. Furthermore, the virtues that Gandhi extolled as the basis of *swaraj* were those associated with the classic Indian wife. Meekness and obedience were the other side of strength and courage. Men were fond of speaking of the "weaker sex," but this was because they lacked understanding of the true meaning of strength. The female sex is "the nobler of the two, for it is the embodiment of sacrifice, silent suffering, humility, faith and knowledge. . . . A woman's intuition has often proved superior to man's arrogant assumption of superior knowledge."[21]

Gandhi was appealing to the masses of Indian women, but the ones who responded most strongly, and who were able to play a part in political life perhaps unmatched by that of women anywhere else in the world, were women of the upper and middle classes. Women provided a reservoir of intelligence and skill that had never before been tapped for the national cause, and thousands of women found release from the stultifying boredom of the routines of upper-class Indian life by throwing themselves into the Gandhian movement. They became his most ardent disciples, providing him with unpaid assistants for organizational work and stirring society by their willingness to march in possessions and go to jail. Their reward was high office and influence.

As with all aspects of the development of the nationalist movement, the activity of the Indian leaders was only part of the picture; the response of the government was crucial in defining its form and direction. The acquiscent attitude of the government that emerged in the months after the program of non-cooperation was announced in September 1920 was regarded by many British officials—and also by the many Indians who still gave their full support to the British—as a sign of weakness that encouraged disloyalty. When Gandhi said, "Non-cooperators are at war with the Government, they have declared rebellion against it," the case for his arrest seemed clear. But the government held back from arresting him, for despite the Rowlatt Acts, the government moved within a legal framework that required actual proof of criminal action. Gandhi had used a vocabulary that implied rebellion, but he had not in fact broken the law. The government was anxious not to make a martyr of Gandhi and the other leaders.

Civil Disobedience

During the last months of 1921 there was an increase of violence throughout India. How much of this was the product of the noncooperation program is hard to say, but in many instances it clearly grew out of deep-seated local frustrations and tensions that found an outlet in the nationalist movement. Within the Indian National Congress itself there was growing dissatisfaction over Gandhi's reluctance to initiate full-scale civil disobedience throughout the nation. Gandhi hesitated but finally agreed that each province should make its own plans for starting mass civil disobedience, including the refusal to pay taxes; but he insisted that all those who participated should first pledge themselves to non-violence, hand-spinning, Muslim-Hindu unity, and the eradication of discrimination against the lowest castes, the "untouchables." Behind the pledge was his fear of what might happen once the campaign got under way. He wanted its advocates to realize that "Mass civil disobedience is like an earthquake, a sort of general upheaval on the political plane. When the reign of mass civil disobedience begins, there the subsisting Government ceases to function. . . . The police stations, the court offices, etc., all shall cease to be Government property, and shall be taken over by the people."[22]

Finally Gandhi gave the word: Mass civil disobedience would start on January 31, 1922, but it would begin with a trial in the district of Bardoli in Bombay led by Gandhi himself. Even at this point he held off, giving the governor general a chance to prevent civil disobedience by showing his change of heart through releasing political prisoners and restoring the freedom of the press. The country had followed all these steps with mounting tension, and when the governor general's refusal came, Gandhi's followers were ready for decisive action.

But just at this moment word reached Gandhi of an outbreak of violence in the village of Chauri Chaura in the United Provinces. A group of noncooperators who had been harassed by the police surrounded the police station and set fire to it. Twenty-two of the policemen were either burned alive or were killed by the mob as they tried to escape. Gandhi was horrified by the brutality of the incident and, in his own language, concluded that "God spoke clearly through Chauri Chaura. . . . He has warned me . . . that there is not yet in India that non-violent and truthful atmosphere which alone can justify mass civil disobedience." He issued an order calling off the whole campaign. His followers, many of whom were in jail, were dumbfounded at this abrupt reversal, especially after Gandhi's ultimatum a few days before to the governor general declaring that civil disobedience would begin unless the government changed its policies. Gandhi admitted that this was "the bitterest cup of humiliation to drink," but it was the voice of Satan, he said, that appealed to his pride by reminding him of his "pompous threats to the Government and promises to the people of Bardoli." Not to call off the movement was to deny the truth.[23]

Jawaharlal Nehru tells how those who, like himself, were in prison reacted with amazement and resentment to the news of

Gandhi's action. Thousands of people were ready to go to prison for their political beliefs, and the whole country was responding in excitement and expectation to Gandhi's plans. Suspending civil disobedience just when it seemed to be on the point of making an impact on the nation seemed inexplicable. It was, however, the product of something more than a quixotic intuition. His religious idiom suggested that his main concern was the inviolate purity of the doctrine of nonviolence as a political technique, but behind this was a shrewd assessment of the realities of Indian life. The violent episode at Chauri Chaura had convinced him that he must go slowly, for he knew that the poverty and frustrations of Indian life made violence endemic. He was an anarchist in his view of the perfect society, but he had no expectation that the mere destruction of the existing order could lead to anything but new forms of tyranny. He had meant what he had said, he insisted, when he promised that *swaraj* could come in a year, but only if there was a change of heart on the part of the people. From the standpoint of his ethical theories, the pervasive violence of the past year had shown that the people were not yet ready for the purifying experience of *satyagraha*, of civil disobedience conducted without violence even under the severest provocation.

The success of Gandhi in identifying non-violence as the peculiar characteristic of Indian life, in the minds of Indians as well as foreigners, has tended to mask an aspect of Indian life that is of the greatest importance to modern Indian political life, nemely the frequency of outbreaks of violence. While we do not possess the kind of historical data that would permit us to say with assurance that there was less violence in previous periods of Indian history than there was after 1920, it seems reasonably clear that there has been more of what is referred to as "communal violence," that is, outbreaks where the targets of attack are other religious groups. Many nationalist leaders at the time had the easy explanation that the riots were engineered by the British as part of the strategy of "Divide and Rule" to prevent Muslims and Hindus from uniting in a common front. Aside from the lack of any real proof of this having happened, it is hard to believe that they would have taken the enormous risks of creating an unconrollable situation. Nor is there any evidence that, as often suggested by foreign observers, that Hindus and Muslims harbour undying hatreds for each other for historic and religious reasons. While such antagonisms were undoubtedly appealed to, the violence of the pre-independence period, as in the post-independence period, seems explainable to a large extent by a number of factors that are part of the reality of modern Indian life that were not present to the same extent in earlier times.

One such factor is a sense of change, carrying with it new possibilities, new ways of doing things, and, conversely, dissatisfaction with the old. Especially among young men in a traditional society, with all its conventions and constraints, often responded to these possibilities with the use of violence. Closely related to this was the economic dislocation and unemployment occasioned by the end of the war, and, especially in the Punjab, with the return of thousands of demobilized soldiers. But the most important factor was undoubtedly the new electoral politics, in which, politicians in India as elsewhere, saw the advantages in appealing for support to groups or communities, and these were usually identifiable through religious designations. Especially in the cities, another factor in the riots were members of the under- world culture, known in India as "goondas," men living on the margins of society who were available to stir up violence and to profit from it. To all of this explosive mix, an appeal to religion gave a potent legitimacy, for whatever the actual motivations or causes of a violent outbreak, actions, however horrendous, could be condoned on the grounds that the righteous cause had to be defended against the onslaughts of evil.

The working out of these factors in a variety of combinations can be seen in a number of incidents in the 1920's. The most serious outbreak of violence since 1857 came on the Malabar coast, where what can be seen in one reading simply as a classic case of peasants rising and killing oppressive landlords. But the rebelling peasants were Muslims and the landlords were Hindu, so the affair had from the beginning a religious coloration of Hindu against Muslims, as well as rich against poor. In the Punjab, there were tensions, although not a great deal of actual violence when in events that foreshadowed the 1980's, a group of militant Sikhs denounced the older generation of Sikhs for having made too many concessions to Hindu practices, and demanded a purifying of the leadership of the religious shrines and temples. In Bihar and the United Provin- ces there were frequent clashes over such matters as the slaughter of cows by Muslims and the playing of music in front of mosques by Hindus on Muslim holy days. This whole volatile situation was in the background, then, when Gandhi called off the first civil disobedience movement.

Gandhi's Arrest

Gandhi was also aware, as many of his followers were not, that behind the facade of political unity the noncooperation movement was rapidly disintegrating. With most of the ablest leaders in jail, it would be without direction. The Muslim leaders saw little chance of gains for their particular interests from Gandhi's tactics, and as Turkey itself moved to destroy the power of the caliph, the whole Khilafat issue, which had been used so skillfully by Gandhi two years before to forge an alliance, was now of little importance. And on the simple level of organization, always of the greatest concern to Gandhi as a practical politician, the Indian National Congress showed signs of serious weakness that would make a long struggle difficult. Gandhi had emphasized that he would need complete cooperation; what he was demanding was complete obedience. He now knew that the majority of the leaders were no longer with him and that the enormous popularity he enjoyed among the masses was very often based upon a false image of his power and his intention. "I know that the only thing that the Government dreads," he wrote, "is this huge majority I seem to command. They little know that I dread it even more than they." He was a prisoner of the violence and frustration that had found a focus in the nationalist movement, and by this time he was "actually and literally praying for a disastrous defeat."[24] The obvious defeat would be his arrest. In his own religious terminology this would be a purification; in political terms it would give him time to redefine his purposes and regroup his forces for another noncooperative movement.

Gandhi was not arrested until March 10, 1922, and the governor general's delay was justified, for his action aroused none of the violence that might have followed if Gandhi had been arrested earlier. At his trial Gandhi pleaded guilty to the charge of preaching disaffection to the government. In passing sentence on March 18, 1922, Justice Broomfield acknowledged that Gandhi was

In a different category from any person I have ever tried or
am likely to have to try . . . In the eyes of millions of your
countrymen, you are a great patriot and a great leader. Even
those who differ from you in politics look upon you as man of
high ideals and of noble and even saintly life.[25]

*   *   *

The first chapter of the Gandhian era of Indian politics ended
with the Indian National Congress in disorganized confusion, its
leaders in jail, and the noncooperation movement, which had
preempted the loyalties and energies of the nationalists for two
years, suspended. Each of the subsequent compaigns was to end
similarly. But the movement had opened up Indian society to the
nationalist cause, and Gandhi could use the symbols of defeat as
well as those of success for his appeal. Jawaharlal Nehru, in
trying to explain Gandhi's hold over intellectuals like himself
and hard-headed, skeptical politicians like his father, once spoke
of those qualities of Gandhi which had a universal appeal: his
steely will, the combination of humility and controlled power, his
ability to hold an audience. But beyond this was the way the
masses reacted to his spell. Many foreigners also reacted to that
spell, of course, but there was often a fulsome condescension in
their praise that was absent in the reaction of the Indian masses.
In his skillful use of the values and symbols of the Indian tradition,
he dramatized himself as the embodiment of the nation, even
while, undoubtedly with perfect sincerity, he denigrated the personal acclaim. An important element in this ability to appeal to
the tradition was his long period of separation from it in England
and South Africa. Only someone who was wholly immersed in
the tradition, and yet who had looked at it from the outside, could
have used it so intuitively. Thus the prison sentence became part
of the drama of renunciation and suffering he envisaged as the way
India must follow to find true freedom. Prison became the sub-
stitute for the banishment to the forest that plays the central role
in so many of the great legends of India, where the hero accepts
the sentence gracefully and turns the forest into a spiritual retreat
from which he returns strengthened and purified.

Gandhi emerged from prison in 1924 confident that the future
was with him, not with those who were seeking to redirect the

nationalist movement back into the old channels through participation in the legislative assemblies and other institutions set up
by the administration. For the next twenty years the tensions
between the two interpretations—the Gandhian insistence on social
salvation through personal commitment as opposed to the policies
of institutional participation—governed the development of Indian
nationalism.

NOTES

[1]Great Britain, *Parliamentary Papers*, 1918, Vol. 8, "Indian Constitutional
Reforms," pp. 113-114.

[2]Quoted in B.R. Nanda, *Mahatma Gandhi* (London: Allen & Unwin, 1958),
p. 153.

[3]Quoted in Jawaharlal Nehru, *An Autobiography* (Bombay: Allied Publishers, 1962), p. 46

[4]Quoted in Nanda, *Mahatma*, p. 159.

[5]*Satyagraha* pledge of February 24, 1919, in D.G. Tendulkar, *Mahatma*, 8
vols. (New Delhi: Publications Division, Government of India, 1960), Vol. I, p.
241.

[6]Quoted in *ibid.*, p. 258.

[7]Rabindranath Tagore, *Nationalism* (New York: Macmillan, 1917), p. 133.

[8]Tagore to Gandhi, April 12, 1919, in Tendulkar, *Mahatma*, Vol. I, p. 259.

[9]Mohandas K. Gandhi, *An Autobiography*, M. Desai (tr.) (Boston: Beacon
Press, 1959), p. 470.

[10]Quoted in Nanda, *Mahatma*, p. 180.

[11]Gandhi, in *Young India*, June 16, 1920, quoted in Tendulkar, *Mahatma*,
Vol. I, p. 355.

[12]Quoted in Nanda, *Mahatma*, p. 205.

[13]Tendulkar, *Mahatma*, Vol. II, pp. 10-11.

[14]Tagore to C.F. Andrews, March 13, 1921, quoted in John Broomfield,
Elite Conflict in a Plural Society (Berkeley: University of California Press, 1968),
p. 150.

[15]Tagore, "The Call to Truth" in de Bary, *Sources of Indian Tradition*, p.
794.

[16]*Ibid.*, pp. 795-796:

[17]Sir William Vincent, minutes of October 10, 1921, quoted in Nanda,
Mahatma, p. 225.

[18]Nehru, *Autobiography*, p. 69.

[19]Quoted in Tendulkar, *Mahatma*, Vol. II, p. 55.

[20]Gandhi, in *Young India*, October 13, 1921.

[21]Quoted in Tendulkar, *Mahatma*, Vol. II, p. 50.

[22]Gandhi at Congress meeting, Delhi, November 4 1921, quoted in *ibid*, p. 66

[23]Gandhi, in *Young Inaia*, February 16, 1922, quoted in *ibid.*, p. 111.

[24]Gandhi, in *Young India*, March 2, 1922, quoted in *ibid.*, p. 122.

[25]Quoted in Philips, *The Evolution of India and Pakistan*, p. 224.

5
The Politics of Right Mistakes

The excitement generated by the noncooperation program from 1920 to 1922 was followed by a period of frustration and indecision. The optimistic slogan of "*swaraj* in a year" was mocked by Gandhi's abrupt ending of civil disobedience. And with most of the nationalist leaders in jail, there was little hope of reviving the agitation. Yet the government did not really profit from the failure of the first Gandhian assault. The new constitution, which had seemed so radical to many British politicians, had been almost universally condemned in India for its timidity in moving the country toward responsible government. There was widespread unrest throughout the country leading to numerous violent outbreaks, of which the Hindu-Muslim riots were the most publicized example. Economic depression added to the general malaise that characterized public life in the 1920s. There were, nonetheless, developments during the period that moved India toward *swaraj* in the Gandhian sense of national integration and a growth in self-respect, although by very different paths from those he envisaged. Despite the hostile reception that the new constitution had received, the legislative assemblies promoted forms of political participation that became the basis for the development of a successful system of party government. At the same time, India also became involved in the international political community in ways that defined her national existence in the eyes of the rest of the world, while giving the nationalist movement itself a new perspective.

India's International Status

India's changed international status was a direct outcome of her contribution to the Allied cause during World War I, for even though her external affairs were wholly under the control of Great Britain, she was one of the signatories of the Treaty of Versailles. This made her automatically a member of the League of Nations under the first clause of the Covenant, which assigned original membership to the signatories of the treaty, despite the fact that she would have been excluded by the second clause, which confined membership to self-governing states.

The anomaly of India being recognized as an independent state by the international community and yet being denied responsible government in internal affairs became a sore point with Indians of all political persuasions. The members of the new Liberal Foundation, the old Congress moderates, were probably more sensitive to the indignities inherent in the ambiguities of India's international situation than were the more radical nationalists. Being products of an educational system and an intellectual milieu that had made them outward looking and responsive to the political values of the Western world, the liberals attributed great importance to India's identity as an autonomous nation in a world setting. India's failure to secure a permanent seat in the League Council and to be given proportionate representation in the Secretariat was especially galling to them, linking their sympathies with the rest of the Indian nationalist movement, even though they dissented from the direction it had taken since the advent of Gandhi. But despite these slights, membership in the League of Nations gave her representation in many international bodies, particularly in the influential International Labour Organization. The Indians who attended international meetings were usually men of great ability, such as Srinivasa Sastri, who made India visible in a new and impressive way to the diplomats and civil servants of the West. Within the British Empire itself India was given more or less the same status as the dominions at the various imperial conferences that were called in the 1920s. Participation in the League of Nations and other international bodies meant that in theory and in fact India was not a "new" nation in 1947 ; it also gave her a nucleus of officials experienced in diplomatic negotiations.

The treatment of Indians abroad was an immediate link between internal political concerns and India's new status as a member of the international community. During the nineteenth century hundreds of thousands of Indians had gone to work in Burma, Ceylon, Malaya, South Africa, the Fiji Islands, and the West Indies. Many of these were indentured laborers, attracted by promises of passage and high wages from the poverty of rural Indian life. The result was that by the 1920s nearly two million Indians were living abroad, almost all in British colonies or dominions. Substandard housing, low wages, lack of educational facilities, high mortality rates, and widespread prostitution, due to the low proportion of women to men, combined with social discrimination to make their condition of special concern to Indian reformers. In South Africa the discrimination was legal, with Indians being prevented by law from acquiring land outside specified locations. But despite the many disabilities imposed upon them, Indians had prospered in South Africa as elsewhere, and it was this prosperity, as well as their very real difficulties, that had made it possible for them to bring their case before the Indian public.

Gandhi had, of course, been the most effective spokesman for the cause of Indians abroad during his career in South Africa. He and his friends had won a sympathetic hearing from the government of India, which recognized that the question of Indians abroad had explosive political consequences. The government of India reported to the secretary of state that the question of the treatment of indentured laborers was the cause of more bitterness than any other issue in Indian politics.

An act to forbid the recruiting of indentured labor in India was passed in 1916, but the system was not finally abolished until 1920, and still indignities lingered. In the history of Indian nationalism, overseas Indians served the same function that minority groups had served elsewhere : a source of irritation for the host country and a focus of indignation for nationalist sentiment at home.

Another aspect of the emigration problem was the right of Indians to enter "white" British dominions, particularly Canada and Australia. The numbers involved were minuscule, but the situation came to be of passionate concern to Indian nationalists in the 1920s as India received recognition in the League of Nations and in the British Empire on a level of equality with the self-governing dominions. Since as British subjects Indians could claim access to the dominions, special discriminatory regulations were necessary to exclude them. This discrimination against Indians overseas by other countries of the empire was an important factor in the anti-Western sentiment that became obvious after the end of World War I. This was pointed out by a correspondent of the London *Times* in 1922, when he deplored what he called "the most distressing feature of the whole situation," the fact that "behind all immediate grievances and discontents, whether Caliphate, Sikh, or Non-cooperationist, there is a continual growth of racial antagonism."[1]

India's needs and aspirations were also shown in the 1920s by a renewed interest in the economic basis of nationhood. In general this continued the emphasis of the earlier nationalists on the economic disadvantages India suffered by being compelled to be a supplier of raw materials to the industrialized West. But the specific grievance was the tariff structure. The British government had insisted throughout the nineteenth century that tariffs be kept at a minimum, despite the obvious disadvantage this gave to the development of industries in India, and in opposition to the government of India's desire to use import duties as a means of raising needed revenues. For Indian nationalists this was evidence, as one newspaper put it, "how Englishmen are blinded by selfishness ; how in their anxiety to protect the interests of their own countrymen, they do not even hesitate to injure the interests of others—to draw the knife, so to speak, across other people's throats."[2]

The framers of the 1919 constitution had recognized the resentment over tariffs as one of the stumbling blocks to the working of the reforms. The inescapable conclusion, according to a parliamentary committee, was that India should have fiscal autonomy, so that she could make tariff arrangements fitted to her needs. The recommendations of the official commission followed the economic thinking of the nationalist leaders for the previous forty years : There should be a policy of protection for selected industries and the elimination of export duties. The change in India's relation to world markets was indicated by the fact that the competition was no longer with the English cotton manufacturers, but with the Japanese. The long struggle for fiscal autonomy in one sphere was thus won long before political independence was achieved. Such a victory lacked the drama of the political arena, but it was of great importance in the process of defining India as a national unit.

Division in Nationalist Movement

In more strictly political terms the focus of nationalist interest was the question of participation in the second election for the legislative councils in 1923. The underlying issue was whether Gandhi and his program would still dominate the Indian National Congress, which would mean refusal to participate in the elections, or whether there would be a return to a more normal pattern of political activity, with Congress leaders running for office. The conflict was solved in one of the compromises typical of Indian nationalist history. When their proposal to contest the elections was voted down by those who remained loyal to Gandhi, C.R. Das and Motilal Nehru resigned and formed the Swaraj party. The Congress then voted to permit those who had no conscientious objections to participating in the elections to do so, while the others should continue the Gandhian program of social work with the masses. The Swarajists, for their part, agreed that if their method failed, they would join a new civil disobedience campaign.

The Swaraj party, representing the Indian National Congress in everything but name, emerged as the largest single political party and the only one with anything approaching an all-Indian organization. Yet it by no means won sweeping victories. Only in the Central Provinces, an area relatively lacking in a history of political activity, did the Swarajists win a clear-cut majority. With about one-third of the 145 seats, they dominated the central Legislative Council ; and in Bengal, Bombay, and the United Provinces, three areas of vital political importance, their bloc of votes was often a decisive force. The Liberal Federation had won many seats in 1920, but in 1923 they lost most of them through the opposition of the Swarajists.

In later nationalist version of Indian history, the Liberals tend at this point to disappear from the story, but in fact, despite their small representation in the legislature, they continued to have a very important part in Indian national development. They were respected by the government, and although sometimes denounced as collaborators by the nationalists, they frequently provided liaison between the nationalists and the officials. They were also

the spokesmen for many Indians, especially those in official positions, who by either temperament or status were unlikely to be
attracted by the Gandhian ideology with its austerity and its
rejection of industrialism and the modern world. Large numbers
of this class were never overtly identified with the nationalist movement, but the Liberals gave them at least a semblance of political
representation.

Another important result of the elections in 1923, as in 1921,
was the victory in Madras of the Justice party, a reminder that the
content of Indian nationality must not be equated with the Indian
National Congress. The Justice party was distinctive in that it
represented the hostility of the non-Brahmans, who made up 95
percent of the population, toward the age-old dominance of the
Brahmans in social and political life. The leaders of the movement were not from the most economically and socially oppressed
classes, but were those with some economic and political power
who resented the Brahman monopoly in such crucial areas as
education and the public services. The Justice party also spoke
for a kind of nascent subnationalism—the South with its Dravidian
languages, especially Tamil, against the North, with its Indo-Aryan
languages. The Indian National Congress was suspect, because its
leaders in the South, as in the North, were mainly from the
Brahman caste or other high castes. In this situation the possibility was present for the development of a regional nationalism that
would challenge the claim of the Congress as the spokesman for
an Indian nationalism that embraced the whole country. That
this kind of regionalism, which became such a potent factor in
Indian political life after 1947, was not stronger in the South in
the 1920s was due to the internal weaknesses of the Justice party
itself, as well as to the lack of cultural homogeneity in Madras.
The province included not only the Tamil-speaking majority, but
also millions of Telegu speakers and substantial numbers of other
language groups. The Justice party had no program or ideological
position, apart from its anti-Brahmanical stance, on which to base
an appeal. Furthermore, the Justice party's opposition to the
Congress made it generally pro-British, or at least pro-government,
a handicap in a situation where nationalism was increasingly identified with a commitment to ending British rule.

Because the system of dyarchy, with responsibility for government divided between the nominated governor and the elected

ministers, applied only to the provincial governments, not to the central Legislative Council, the provinces became the major centers of political activity and interest. Decentralization had been one of the objectives of the 1919 constitution, and as the provincial governments became more important and their decisions became of greater popular concern, provincial politics provided the nationalist leaders with their sphere of influence, rather than the all-India setting of the earlier phases of the nationalist movement. This provincial setting was a significant factor in the weakening of the power and prestige of the Indian National Congress during the mid-twenties. Therefore, to some extent the new constitutional experiment worked against the continued growth of a generalized nationalist sentiment. By having provided the political leaders with provincial, rather than national, forums, dyarchy gave modern institutional form to the cultural and linguistic regionalism that had seemed to many observers to be the distinctive characteristic of India.

This strengthening of regionalism made a vital contribution, however, to Indian nationhood and the sense of nationality by forcing Indian politicians to deal with the realities of administrative power and by forcing the bureaucracy to think and act politically. In the fifteen years in which the new system functioned with varying degrees of success in different provinces, the normal patterns of administration were maintained and new ones initiated, such as the vote for women, compulsory education in some areas, and the encouragement of local self-government on the village level.

The transitional nature of dyarchy made the system peculiarly frustrating to Indian nationalists in the 1920s. There was an air of impermanence about it, with a promise for change explicit in the whole constitutional framework, and the nationalists were anxious to have this pledge redeemed. The problem for them, as for the government, was to find a method. When they entered the provincial councils, their goals had been clear : Through unrelenting opposition to all government measures, they were to bring about a revision of the constitution that would replace dyarchy with genuine responsible government. The government argued that it was precisely this attitude that made the advance to responsible government impossible, since the purpose of the constitutional experiment had been to provide training in ministerial responsibility to the elected representatives of the people.

The search for nationhood had reached the point where fundamental decisions had to be made about the direction which would
be taken by the Indian National Congress. The Swarajists were
arguing for a political solution based on compromise and negotiation, set within the framework of political realities as defined by
the transitional 1919 constitution. Gandhi was insistent upon his
vision of an India that had no need for such compromises. For
the realization of his vision, however, Gandhi needed the Congress,
including the energy and intelligence represented by the Swarajists,
and he fought to prevent the Swarajists from pursuing policies that
would alienate them from the Congress in the same way the Liberals
had been alienated.

Without any positive platform, weakened by resignations and
lack of support from Gandhi and the Congress organization, the
Swaraj party virtually disintegrated in the elections of 1926. Its
place was taken by various other groups, most of whom were
short-lived as political entities, but whose formation showed the
growing divergences within the nationalist movement. Gandhi
watched the factional struggles but made little attempt at this point
at reconciliation. He regarded the question of elections to the
councils as irrelevant to his main concern—the political education
of the masses—and he was content to let the parties destroy each
other. His own role was clear in his mind : "I must hold myself
in reserve, till the storm is over and the work of rebuilding has
commenced."[3]

While he waited, Gandhi's own energies and those of his
closest disciples went into what he called the "constructive program" in contrast to the work of those who entered the councils
and engaged in political activities on the national and provincial
level. He asked in 1927 : "How many of us can take a direct
part in the working of that programme? . . . How many of us are
entitled to elect members to these legislative bodies? Are the
millions of villagers enfranchised ? . . . What then is the programme
that can weld together the thirty crores [300 million] of people
scattered on a surface 1,900 miles long and 1,500 miles broad in
700,000 villages ?"[4] When Strachey and the others pondered this
question, they did so rhetorically. They believed that nothing
could unite India. For Gandhi there was "one simple and unequivocal answer . . . the spinning wheel and khaddar [homes-

pun.]"[5] For this reason he watched, with some satisfaction, as the political parties fought each other in the councils.

One of the groups that helped destroy the Swaraj party as an effective political force was a coalition headed by two of the most famous of the older generation of leaders from the Indian National Congress, M. M. Malaviya and Lala Lajpat Rai. They spoke for a strong faction within the Congress that felt that the interests of the Hindu majority, as opposed to those of Muslims, had not been properly protected by the Swarajists in the legislative councils. They did not represent a new movement within the Congress so much as one that had been quiescent since the Lucknow Pact of 1916 and the Khilafat movement of the early 1920s. B. G. Tilak's vigorous emphasis on the importance of the Hindu elements of Indian culture had been muted in the years when Gandhi was making common cause with the Muslims, but there had always been segments of the nationalist movement that felt the Hindu heritage had been betrayed by excessive concessions to the Muslims, on the one hand, and to Western secular ideas, on the other.

The Hindu Mahasabha had been formed to safeguard the Hindu way of life in 1906, but it did not come into prominence until the 1920s. It was not a political party and did not run candidates for elections, but it included many members from the Congress, with Malaviya and Lajpat Rai among its leaders. The revival and strengthening of the Hindu Mahasabha in the midtwenties and its very considerable accession of power within the Indian National Congress were related to the worsening of the Hindu-Muslim relations, perhaps the most significant feature of Indian political and social life in the period.

By the mid-twenties Hindu-Muslim riots had become commonplace. Charges that the riots were caused by British *agents provocateurs* were often made but have never been proved, and in any case the British could not have created the violence had there not been deeply rooted antagonisms. As suggested in an earlier chapter, these antagonisms became visible in the late nineteenth century as a nationalist ideology was articulated, with its inevitable appeals to religion, language, culture, and history, all of which were divisive, not cohesive, forces for Hinduism and Islam. The emergence of Gandhi sharpened these distinctions, despite the fact that he was an adamant spokesman for Hindu-Muslim solidarity. On the one hand, by making the Khilafat movement central to the nationalist cause in 1920, he had, despite all his disclaimers to the contrary, emphasized the importance of being a Muslim, rather than an Indian, nationalist. For both Hindus and Muslims it indicated the primacy of religious identifications in Indian social life. Even more important, and again despite Gandhi's denial that this was the increasing use of an essentially Hindu vocabulary of politics. Gandhi's extraordinary empathy with the Hindu masses depended upon the formulation of a nationalist ideology in terms that were comprehensible to them. The corollary was that this nationalism became less appealing to Muslims, especially to the Muslim intellectuals who did not have the instinctive response to the Gandhian ideology that the Hindu intelligentsia had.

The direct result of the worsening of Hindu-Muslim relations was the attempt by M. A. Jinnah to revitalize the Muslim League and make it an active political force. It had been moribund since the start of the Khilafat movement, which had absorbed the energies of the Muslim political leaders. But after he had left the Indian National Congress over the non-cooperation and civil disobedience issues, Jinnah saw the possibility of using the League as a pressure group to gain constitutional protection for the Muslim minority. He succeeded in drawing the League together again as a functioning political organisation, but it had no popular support from the masses or from the religious leaders, many of whom regarded Jinnah and his followers as heretical modernists. In addition, the League itself was divided by internal quarrels. The opportunity to make the League a more powerful force in Indian politics came at the end of the 1920s in connection with the appointment by the British government of the Simon Commission to examine the need for further constitutional changes in India.

First Demand for Independence

It is ironical that the announcement of the Simon Commission in 1927 brought new life to the Indian nationalist movement on all levels, breaking the spirit of malaise and frustration brought on by the divisions within the Congress and the viciousness of the Hindu-Muslim rioting. The 1919 constitution had made provision for reviewing its effectiveness after ten years. But the British Conservatives appointed the commission, headed by Sir John Simon, two years early, because they feared that the nationalist cause would gain too much sympathy if the Labour party took power. Indian leaders of all political views had been demanding a commission for some time, but when Indians were not included as members, the Simon Commission was denounced as a new insult to Indian national life. Political India had found a common cause once more, and India's search for nationhood took on a new sense of urgency.

The older generation of nationalists, including Gandhi, who found it difficult to visualize an India that was not in some way related to Great Britain, argued that dominion status for India was the limit of realistic possibilities. By 1928, however, there was a group of young men within the Indian National Congress demanding that full independence should be the stated aim of the Congress. The leaders in this revolt were Jawaharlal Nehru, the son of Motilal, and Subhas Chandra Bose, a young Bengali who aspired to the position of leadership once held by C. R. Das. They brought fresh ideas and new vitality into the Congress, for both had been influenced by contemporary European socialist and Marxist thought, and, more than any other of the Congress leaders, they saw Indian politics in terms of ideology. But despite Nehru's socialism and his distaste for religious symbols, he was always drawn emotionally toward Gandhi in a way that Bose never was. And from the very beginning Gandhi recognized that Nehru's ideological positions were far more flexible than those of Bose, whose allegiances and sympathies with the revolutionary tradition of Bengali politics were a barrier to wholehearted acceptance of the Gandhian program, with its ethic of nonviolence.

The divergence between the political understanding of Nehru and Bose and that of Gandhi came to a head over the Congress' position on India's future constitutional relationship with Great Britain. Nehru and Bose, with strong support from within the Congress, demanded that India's goal should be complete independence, not dominion status. By the end of 1928 it seemed that a split in the Congress was inevitable, so sharply had the issue divided the party. But Gandhi once more devised a formula for compromise: They would ask for dominion status, but if it were not granted by the end of 1929, then the Congress would begin a new civil disobedience movement. This not only prevented a division within the Congress, but it also brought Gandhi back into full participation in political life, for when the British did not agree to grant dominion status, Gandhi began a new civil disobedience campaign.

The second civil disobedience campaign began in March 1930, eight years after the collapse of the first one. Gandhi proceeded cautiously, despite the impatience and enthusiasm of the supporters, as he was still uncertain that the masses were ready for the kind of movement he envisaged. The educated classes had independence as their slogan, but at one time Gandhi had defied anyone to give him a translation of the word "independence" in any Indian language that would be intelligible to the masses. What they needed was some symbol that touched their daily lives. He found it in the salt laws, which made the manufacture of salt a government monopoly. Gandhi's argument was that the laws were unjust, since they increased the price of commodity that is a necessity of life. Gandhi's method for breaking the salt laws was dramatic and appealing. It began with a march from his headquarters near Ahmedabad in Gujarat to the seacoast at Dandi, 240 miles away, where salt was manufactured from seawater.

The breaking of the salt laws at Dandi was the signal for the beginning of civil disobedience throughout the country, and the government soon took action. Numerous outbreaks of violence took place. The Indian National Congress accused the police of provocation, but the government placed the blame on the attacks of mobs on government and private property. Many people were killed, and thousands arrested, including all the leaders of the Congress. Most of those jailed were ordinary members of the party or people involved in the riots, but they also included men of wealth and and power such as the Nehrus. Gandhi himself was not arrested until May 1930, since the government was afraid his imprisonment would evoke a new round of disorders.

The civil disobedience campaign continued for six months more, but with the leaders in jail there was little hope for an organized movement. Gandhi began conversations with the governor general through the mediation of the Liberal leaders. Gandhi's announcement that, in return for concessions from the government, the second civil disobedience compaign had been suspended came as a blow to his followers; after refusing to negotiate the previous year, he seemed to have given in now for very minor concessions. There was no mention of dominion status, much less independence, but only a concern with what seemed to many of them minor items: the release of prisoners, the calling of a round-table conference, the permission for peaceful picketing of liquor shops, and the right of those who lived near the sea to make their own salt. Nineteen-thirty had been, as Nehru put it, "a wonder year," when the whole country seemed willing to follow Gandhi's bidding in resisting the British. Now once more, as in 1922, Gandhi seemed to have let his followers down, just when they might have shaken British power.

At this point of low morale, the nationalist movement found a martyr in Bhagat Singh, a young Sikh revoluntionary, who was found guilty of a political murder. The extraordinary popularity he achieved was embarrassing to the Congress' leaders, who were committed to the position that Indians had accepted the ideal of nonviolence. But the emotional response that Bhagat Singh's cause engendered was a useful antidote to the pessimism and frustration that followed the ending of the civil disobedience campaign. When Bhagat Singh and his accomplices were hanged, riots broke out in which hundreds of people were killed and wounded. And although Gandhi deplored the violence, he extolled Bhagat Singh's bravery and sacrifice. His attitude at such times often confused his admirers in the West, many of whom were Christian pacifists, but for Gandhi the willing sacrifice of blood by the innocent was a necessary foundation for a strong nation. "I would not flinch," he once declared, "from sacrificing even a million lives for India's liberty."[6] But though he was fascinated by the metaphors of martyrdom, with their undertones of purification by blood, this aspect of his thought, as with so much of his ideology, was marked by ambiguity. For example, the actual physical death of martyrdom Gandhi transmuted into the symbolic death of the self through fasting and other austerities.

Hindu-Muslim Relations

The abandonment of the civil disobedience campaign in 1931 marked the end, or at least the postponement, of the debate over dominion status versus independence, one of the two great issues that had arisen out of the Simon Commission. The other issue was the question of Hindu-Muslim relations, which, in terms of the constitutional discussion, was concerned with the guaranteed representation of Muslims in the central and provincial legislative assemblies. Muslim leaders, including Jinnah, had taken an active part in negotiations, but they were convinced that the Congress leadership did not take the issue of Muslim representation seriously. By the end of 1928 Jinnah was beginning to abandon his long attempt to foster cooperation between the Muslim League and the Indian National Congress. Although he was still uncertain of the direction in which he should move, the events of 1929 and 1930, with Gandhi's dramatic exploitation of his following among the Hindu masses, had been decisive for Jinnah. He was convinced that the Muslim League, which so far had failed to elicit either interest among the Muslim masses or unified support from even its own leadership, would have to speak for the Muslims.

At this time Jinnah found a powerful ally in Muhammad Iqbal (1877-1938), the greatest literary figure produced by Indian Muslims in the twentieth century. Jinnah and Iqbal are makers of Pakistan, but they are also makers of Modern India in the sense that its political development after 1930 is not intelligible without considering their work. Jinnah has been assigned the role in Indian nationalist history of the fanatic enemy of Indian unity, building a new nation on hates and fears which he either brought into being or fanned into flames. There is very little to justify this reading of his activities in the 1930s.

Jinnah's insistence that the Muslim community, making up one-quarter of the population of India, constituted a special problem that needed careful constitutional definition was rejected by the Congress leadership for a variety of reasons. Gandhi sought a nation animated by a specific spiritual response, and he was genuinely convinced that this could come from all of India's people, irrespective of their religious identifications, since, as he never wearied of arguing, all religions expressed the same truth. He was probably unaware that this involved a peculiarly Hindu definition of truth. From a different standpoint Nehru and his group rejected religion as a significant factor in modern nationalism, arguing that the tensions leading to Hindu-Muslim riots were rooted in poverty and in the ignorance it produced. Another attitude was represented by men such as M.M. Malaviya, who, deeply Hindu in their outlook and allegiances, saw the Muslim demands not just as a threat to national unity, but also to Hindu culture itself. All of the groups were united in arguing that the Congress was demonstrably neither exclusively Hindu nor anti-Muslim since

many Muslims were active in it, and a number of Muslims had
become presidents of the Congress. Maulana Azad was the most
notable of these "nationalist Muslims," as they became known.
This Muslim support seemed to confirm the Congress' insistence
that it was not a Hindu organization, but the fundamental reality
remained that, however apathetic the Muslim masses might be and
however divided their leadership, the Islamic community in
India possessed all the potentialities to which a nationalist appeal
could be made. This ran counter to the definition of nationalism
with which the Congress had identified itself, but once this alternative nationalism became an option for Indian Muslims, they
were likely to seize upon it as an escape from the political frustrations they shared with other Indians. More than anyone else, it
was Iqbal who articulated the alternative to the Congress' brand
of nationalism.

In his early writings Iqbal had decried nationalism as a disease
of the West that was antithetical to the spirit of Islam, and he
had argued that the Muslims of India would find their salvation
through membership in the whole Islamic community. The failure
of the Khilafat movement and the rise of strong nationalist parties
in many of the Muslim countries turned him inward, and the
course of Indian politics after 1928 convinced him that Indian
Muslims would have to find their true community in some form
of a Muslim state within India. He enunciated this idea for the
first time in 1930 when he was president of the Muslim League.
To the Congress' arguments that religion was not a decisive component in nationality and that Hindus and Muslims could find
solidarity through a common devotion to India, Iqbal answered
that religion and society were organically related in Islam, with
one nourishing the other. "Therefore the construction of a polity
on national lines, if it means a displacement of Islamic principles
of solidarity, is simply unthinkable to a Muslim." Given his
premises, the logic of Iqbal's conclusion was irrefutable. "The
formation of a consolidated North-West Indian Muslim state
appears to me to be the final destiny of the Muslims of at least
North-West India."[7]

Iqbal's arguments were never met in a meaningful way by the
Congress' politicians. Gandhi's answer that all religions could
find fulfillment in the new India since they were guardians of the
same truth, and Nehru's argument that religion was a man's

private concern, having nothing to do with the polity of the state, only strengthened Iqbal's case. While it was true, as Indian nationalists pointed out, that in Western countries different religions and sects lived side by side, united in allegiance to a common nationality, India was different. Hinduism and Islam were not "religions" in the sense that the Western world used the term, Jinnah insisted, but rather were social orders. In the West religious affiliation was one among many aspects of life; in India it denoted the deepest patterns of life and thought. Because of this, as Jinnah put it in a later period, the attempt to meld two basically different social orders into a common nationality "must lead to a growing discontent and final destruction of any fabric that may be so built up for the gnvernment of such a state."[8] Jinnah's point was best understood by the Hindu communal groups; from the opposite end of the political spectrum, they too insisted that in India religion was not, as in the West, one preference among many. Hinduism was the heart of Indian civilization and could not be treated as if it were irrelevant to politics.

Renewal of Nationalist Activity

The problems concerning the nature of Indian nationhood and nationality raised by Iqbal and Jinnah received little attention in 1931. The centre of nationalist concern shifted to London, where Gandhi had gone to attend the round-table conference called as the result of his pact with the government for ending civil disobedience. Gandhi was the sole official representative of the Indian National Congress, and the drama of one man speaking for the most powerful political force in India caught the imagination of the world. For the moment Indian nationality was concentrated in Gandhi. The talks, however, accomplished almost nothing. The British government and the non-Congress delegates wanted to discuss constitutional details, while Gandhi insisted that the only issue was Indian independence.

Gandhi made no attempt to negotiate the details of a constitutional settlement. By this time it was clear that such negotiations were not part of his style of politics. G.K. Gokhale had once remarked on his extraordinary ability to "enchain the attention of the poor man", and to establish "an affinity with the lowly and the distressed." But he had gone on to say: "Be careful that India does not trust him on occasions where delicate negotiations have to be carried on with care and caution . . . acting on the principle that half a loaf is better than no bread."[9] This was a notable insight, but it was only a half-truth, since Gandhi had of course negotiated successfully on numerous occasions. But now Gandhi probably felt the stakes were too high to endanger the country by diverting attention from the main issues: the unity and freedom of India.

When Gandhi returned to India at the end of 1931 another confrontation between the Indian National Congress and the government became inevitable. There had been incidents of terrorism in Bengal, and widespread agitation and rioting elsewhere had been brought on by the worsening economic depression. The government insisted that it had to take strong measures to preserve law and order, including the arrest of Congress leaders who participated in the agitations. Gandhi charged that these measures were in violation of the pact he had made with the governor general before halting the civil disobedience campaign, and he announced plans for its resumption. This time the government acted swiftly, imprisoning Gandhi and the rest of the leaders early in 1932, and declaring the Congress illegal. Civil disobedience continued, however, and the police responded by charging on the crowds that gathered in towns and cities throughout the country. Many people were killed and wounded, and more than 100,000 people were arrested. None of the previous campaigns had elicited such widespread support, and there were many acts of individual defiance that thrilled the country, as when Nehru's mother was beaten by the police after she had placed herself at the head of a procession.

The behaviour of the police at such times caused special bitterness. The government argued that the police had to use force to protect themselves in the face of the mobs, which was probably true. But the reality of the situation was summed up by an Indian observer in a letter to Ramsay MacDonald, the British Labour prime minister.

The police in India, ill-educated, ill-paid, and drawn from the lowest strata of society and accustomed to rough modes, when actually authorised and encouraged to strike persons in the streets, irrespective of station, age or sex, cannot be expected to restrain themselves. Stories of inhuman and barbarous chastisement go about, creating bitterness and racial and com-

munal rancour. Believe me, there will be the very devil to pay
for another generation.[10]

Yet despite the enthusiasm and self-sacrifice, the civil disobedience campaign was not self-sustaining, and by the summer of
1933 most of its vitality was gone. The Indian nationalist movement never had the spirit of a civil war, with its complete commitment occasioned by the knowledge that one was engaged in a fight
to the death in which no quarter would be asked or given. The
processions, the speeches, the newspaper reports, the public
gatherings were made in defiance of government orders, but always
with the assertion that no violence or destruction was intended and
that it was the government which was acting illegally and undemo-
cratically in provoking the riots through the violence of the police.
    The Indian nationalists in 1932 and 1933 were still appealing,
as their predecessors had in the early days of the movement, to
British notions of freedom and legality. The result was that the
repressive legislation and the attacks by the police weakened their
will to resist because they still acknowledged the legitimacy of
British rule.
    The government's policy was probably the major reason for
this exhaustion, but there were other contributing factors. One was
that very important segments of the Indian population actively
opposed the civil disobedience campaign. These included business
and commercial interests and landlords, as well as many intellectuals of moderate political views, such as the leaders of the
Liberals, who were convinced that the time had come for careful
negotiation for a new constitution. The Muslim League was
inactive during these years, but the spirit of malaise that characterized its leadership helped the government, not the Indian
National Congress. Jinnah himself left India for London, feeling
that there was no hope in a united India for the Muslims, who
"were like dwellers in No Man's land; they were either led by
flunkeys of the British Government or the campfollowers of the
Congress."[11] A more complex factor in the weakening of the civil
disobedience movement was Gandhi's activity in prison.
    Gandhi's return to the forefront of India's political conscious-
ness came with his initiation of a series of fasts while he was still in
jail. The first one in September 1932 was a protest against the
British decision to give the untouchables a total of seventy-one

seats in the various provincial legislative councils. The grant was made in response to the demand at the round-table conference of Dr. Bhimrao Ramji Ambedkar, the leader of the untouchables, for the protection of this minority. Gandhi's announcement that he would fast to death unless the award was withdrawn created a dilemma for the British, who feared that Gandhi's death might trigger an outburst of violence the government of India could not contain.

For Gandhi the award of seats to the untouchables, or, as he preferred to call them, the Harijans, God's People, would be a further division of Indian society, perpetuating their inferiority by giving them a vested interest in their low status. Ambedkar denounced this as a thinly veiled argument for using the seventy million untouchables as weightage for the Hindus against the Muslims; but as the attention of the nation focused once more on Gandhi, an intricate agreement was worked out. In essence it assured Harijan representatives twice as many places in the legislative councils but did not give them separate constituencies.

By directing his own attention and that of many of his followers into the campaign against untouchability, Gandhi no doubt drew off some of the energy that might have gone into more directly political purposes, but his concern for what he regarded as an intolerable blot on Hindu society stirred the imagination and the conscience of the Indian people. His ceaseless travels from village to village throughout the country was a paradigm in modern form of the wanderings of the traditional Hindu saint, in quest of salvation both for himself and for those who thronged to see him. Even his insistence that everyone, including the poorest people, should give him some contribution for the national cause was rooted in the elemental feeling that both the giving and receiving of alms are marks of spiritual grace.

Another factor that weighed heavily in Gandhi's decisions at this time was the increasing violence of the crowds, especially in the great northern cities, as they confronted the police. Gandhi did not fear bloodshed and suffering when, according to his beliefs, they could be used creatively, but he feared uncontrolled violence. He was especially troubled by a growing challenge to his conception of the Congress as an organization representating all the interests and classes of the nation. The communists and other left-wing groups were active as participants, if not as leaders, in much

of the violent agitation of 1932 and 1933, and they denounced
Gandhi and the other Congress leaders as the tools of the British
imperialists and the Indian capitalists. Gandhi came to the conclusion that he should retire from the Congress because of his
estrangement from many of the other leaders. His emphasis on the
spinning program and the eradication of untouchability seemed
increasingly irrelevant to those who thought the time had come to
engage in the administration of the country and to fight in the
legislatures for changes in the new constitution the British government had prepared.

1935 India Act

After the second round-table conference had broken up in
1931 without the Indian representatives coming to any agreement
on constitutional safeguards for the minority groups, the British
officials and the government of India proceeded to draft a new
constitution. This was the Government of India Act of 1935, the
last in the long series of British parliamentary acts that since 1773
had defined the nature and power of British rule in India. Despite
the criticism made of it at the time, the act provided the framework
around which the constitution of independent India was built. It
once more asserted the primacy of British rule, but although there
was no specific mention of either dominion status or independence
as future goals, the implicit assumption was that the promise of
1917, the advance toward responsible government, could be fulfilled
within the new framework. It was not a transitional document, as
the 1919 constitution had been; provisions for change and growth
were made, but the act was a definitive solution to what the British
regarded as the major political problems of India.

In general terms the new constitution preserved the ultimate
authority of the governor general as the representative of the
British crown and created a federation in which the princely states
had a considerable degree of autonomy and responsibility. The
system of dyarchy, which had worked in the provinces was to be
introduced at the center, with responsibility for certain aspects of
the administration being turned over to ministers representing the
electors, and others being retained by the governor general. But
since the princes did not accept the proposals made for their

participation, this federal part of the constitution never came into operation. The real changes took place on the provincial level.

The authority of the British government was maintained in the provinces by the governor appointed by the Crown, but the dyarchy of 1919 was abolished. The chief minister would be chosen from the party that commanded the largest majority; the chief minister could then select his own ministers, as in British parliamentary practice. The franchise was given to about 27 percent of the total adult population, including women, making the electorate of thirty-five million one of the largest in the world. The desire to write in safeguards for the rights of minorities led, however, to the fragmentation of this electorate into an extraordinarily complex pattern. There were two kinds of constituencies, general ones and those in which only special classes had a right to vote. Bombay can serve as an example. There were 175 seats in Bombay's Legislative Assembly, with 114 of these for the general population, in effect, for the Hindus. Out of this number fifteen seats were reserved for representatives of the Harijans and other culturally and economically backward Hindu groups. The Muslims were given twenty-nine seats, with the rest divided among tribal peoples, Anglo-Indians, Europeans, Indian Christians, representatives of industry, landowners, universities, labor, and women.

To the British the India Act of 1935 was a generous gesture, meeting all the reasonable demands of the nationalists while safeguarding the rights of the minorities, particularly the Muslims, and ensuring the continued guiding hand of British power. Politically conscious Indians regarded it with disappointment and scorn. It cut across what seemed to be the mainstream of national integration, the process that the British themselves had done so much to further through their centralized administration and modern communications. A federal structure was being created out of an existing unitary government, not as elsewhere from a union of states. The complex franchise, with its constituencies for a multitude of racial, religious, and cultural groups, was subversive of Indian nationality. To men like Nehru the communal franchise was a denial of modernity to India, an attempt to relegate it to the status of Lebanon or the *millets* of the Ottoman Empire. The conviction, long held by the nationalists, that the British accentuated old divisions and created new ones in order to perpetuate their rule was thus strengthened.

The Indian National Congress response was ambiguous. The new constitution was denounced but Congressmen were to contest the elections. They were not to cooperate with the government by taking office, however, if they won a majority of the seats. Instead they were to wreck the new structure from within. When the elections were over, and it was found that the Congress had won majorities in most of the provinces, this decision was changed. On being assured by the governor general that the governor would in normal circumstances exercise his authority only on the advice of the elected ministers, Congress ministers took office in 1937 in seven provinces, including three of the largest and most important, Madras, Bombay, and the United Provinces.

New Strength of the Muslim League

With political power no longer a distant goal to be sought, but a possession to be managed, the stresses that had been apparent for some years became greater. Within the Indian National Congress party itself there was increasing resistance from various groups. One group, led by Subhas Chandra Bose, objected to the dominance of Gandhi and his ideology and the failure, in their view, of the Congress to pursue a socially progressive and anti-imperialist policy. The break came when Bose, having been elected president of the Congress, was forced by Gandhi to resign. Bose then formed a new party, the Forward Bloc. Its manifesto was virtually a rejection of the Congress' commitment to nonviolence and a broadly based consensus. "Only the Left," it declared, "can preserve the revolutionary character of the Congress and bring about an early resumption of the fight for national freedom."[12] Although Bose used the vocabulary of contemporary European socialism, his intellectual and spiritual roots were in the Bengali revolutionary movement. His wartime collaboration with the Nazis was therefore not so much a renunciation of his earlier Marxism as a willingness to use any method to defeat the British. His ardent patriotism, with its atavistic links to religious passion, made an appeal to many Hindus, especially his fellow Bengalis, even if they had no sympathy for his political ideology. The old relationship between religion and nationalism was also seen in the increased activity of the Hindu Mahasabha and allied groups seeking to make Hinduism relevant to the changing political conditions. The reinvigoration of the Muslim League at this time was to a considerable extent a response to this revivalism.

One of the many paradoxes of the history of nationalism in India is that Muslim nationalism, with its explicit grounding in an appeal to a specific religious community, appears to be far less "religious" in its orientation than the nationalism of the Indian National Congress, which very genuinely sought to include Indians of all religious persuasions. Jinnah himself was a rationalist to whom the religious idiom by Gandhi was distasteful, partly because it introduced an irrational element into political discussion, but more importantly because Gandhi had turned the Congress "into an instrument for the revival of Hinduism and for the establishment of Hindu Raj in India."[13]

Jinnah did not strengthen the Muslim League through an appeal to religious emotion. He built his case substantially on the formal recognition by the British in 1909, 1919, and 1935, through the creation of Muslim constituencies, that any political settlement would have to take the Muslims as a subnationality into account. This meant that all decisions on India's future always involved negotiations between the British, the Indian National Congress, and the Muslim League. The Congress had unmistakable claims to be the major beneficiary of the devolution of power, but the League insisted that it was the spokesman for political rights of Muslims that the British as the possessors of power had already acknowledged. Jinnah had a twofold task : to validate the League's claim and to define Muslim political rights in constitutional terms through negotiations between the British and the League.

Although the idea that the Hindus and Muslims constituted two separate nations that might have to find distinct national destinies was suggested at a meeting of the League in 1930, Jinnah did not concentrate on this theoretical argument after the Congress ministries took office in 1937. He took up instead a practical and explosive political issue. This was the charge, made especially in the rural areas, that the Congress ministries were discriminating against Muslims. Although British observers thought that in general the alleged cases of discrimination were rather trivial, truth or falsity in such matters is hard to distinguish. The important fact was that the Muslims felt they were being discriminated against by the Congress. This belief became one of the realities of Indian politics, the focus for fears and frustrations that had their origin in social and economic conditions that had little to do with actual religious status. But just as the leaders of the general nationalist drive for political freedom and national self-identity had often found it necessary to use symbols and vocabulary that were drawn from Hindu culture, so the leaders of the Muslim League had to use the rubric of Islam in order to make its appeal. With a well-articulated social and cultural inheritance to draw upon, the League was able by the 1940s to identify itself with a subnationalism that had to be taken seriously as a possible expression of the aspirations of the Indian Muslims.

*   *   *

The failure of the Indian National Congress to take the Muslim League seriously in the crucial years from 1937 to 1939 has seemed, to many observers, the final political error made by Nehru and Gandhi. The list that critics draw up is long : the refusal to enter the councils in 1920; then, having decided on civil disobedience, the abandonment of it in 1922 and 1934, instead of moving forward to a final confrontation; the unwillingness of the Congress in the 1930s to negotiate details of a constitutional settlement; and the rejection in 1937 of coalition ministries with the League. Other decisions at these climactic moments, it is argued, would have saved India from the turmoil of the 1940s that ended with partition. But what the critics ignore is that the complexity of Indian political and social life would not have permitted any easy transition to responsible government and independence. The decisions made at the time, especially those in which Gandhi had the major influence, do indeed often seem to have been quixotic and mistaken in their understanding of the possibilities of political action. Yet in the total context of India's long effort to define herself as a nation, they were probably the right mistakes. The frustrations and tensions they engendered were related to the fundamental problem in the devolution of power, the answer in explicit political terms to the question Curzon had asked in 1905 ; "Who and what are the real Indian people?"[14] Probably, as the events of the 1940s showed, only a complicated and unsatisfactory answer could be given.

NOTES

[1]London *Times*, March 16, 1922.

[2]Quoted in Bipin Chandra, *The Rise and Growth of Economic Nationalism in India* (New Delhi : People's Publishing House, 1966) P. 239.

[3]Quoted in Tendulkar, *Mahatma*, Vol. II, p. 166.

[4]*Ibid.*, p. 234.

[5]*Ibid.*, p. 244.

[6]*Ibid.*, Vol. III, p. 52.

[7]Muhammad Iqbal, *Speeches and Statements of Iqbal*, "Shamloo" (ed.) (Lahore : Al-Manar Acadmy, 1948), p. 9.

[8]Speech at Lahore, March 23, 1940, quoted in Kahlid B, Sayeed, *The Political System of Pakistan* (Boston : Houghtan Mifflin, 1967), p. 40.

[9]Quoted in M.R. Jayakar, *Story of My Life* (Bombay : Asia Publishing House 1958), Vol. I, 317.

[10]Srinivasa Sastri to Ramsay MacDonald, April 15, 1932, quoted in Kanji Dwarkadas, *India's Fight for Freedom* (Bombay : Popular Prakashan, 1966), p. 416.

[11]Quoted in S.K. Majumdar, *Jinnah and Gandhi* (Calcutta : Firma K.L. Mukhopadhyay, 1966), p. 155.

[12]Subhas Chandra Bose, *Crossroads* (London : Asia Publishing House, 1962). p. 180.

[13]Quoted in Majumdar, *Jinah and Gandhi*, p. 171.

[14]Raliegh, *Lord Curzon in India*, pp. 584-585.

6
End and Beginning

By 1939, despite the frustrations and mistakes of the previous twenty years, a sense of nationality, fused from the disparate elements of India's cultural and political traditions, had become an actuality. Regional differences of language, custom, and historical experience were still as great as they had been in 1880 when Strachey declared it was impossible that men of the Punjab, Bengal and Madras should ever feel they belonged to one great nation. But a change had taken place that even those most committed to the value and necessity of British rule found hard to deny. For large numbers of people throughout the country, and by no means for only those who had been directly influenced by Western education, there was an awareness that being an Indian was part of their essential heritage. They had come to share in what, as was suggested in the first chapter, is one of the fundamental aspects of nationality : the sense that "individual identity hinges on the existence of a national identity," with all the attendant psychological involvement that such an identification entails. The announcement in September 1939 that the governor general had declared India at war on the side of Great Britain and her allies, without prior consultation with Indian political leadership, was thus felt as a personal, as well as a national, slight, requiring a new confrontation with the imperial power.

The pattern of events that followed was a duplication of the earlier confrontations : mutual charges of bad faith, the call for civil disobedience, imprisonments, and finally, agreement on issues that might, it seems, have been reached without the years of frustration and delay. The difference between the new phase, lasting from 1939 to 1947, and the previous ones was that this time there was no real doubt that the final settlement would be Indian independence. The issues had narrowed to questions of timing and methods of devolution of power, even though the language of all the protagonists sometimes concealed this. But the fact that the issues were more precisely defined than they had been in the past did not mean that there was less bitterness or more clarity in regard to solutions that would be acceptable to the three negotiating groups—the British, the Indian National Congress, and the Muslim League. It was true, as the governor general was reminded by a delegation in 1939 representing the Liberal Federation, the Scheduled Castes, and the Hindu Mahasabha, that there were interests in India whom neither the Congress nor the League represented. But these interests carried little weight in the final struggle.

Bargaining for Independence

The Indian National Congress at first offered to support the war effort if the British would make an unequivocal statement that India would get freedom after the war, with an immediate grant of a large measure of responsible government at the central level. When the British replied that such a transfer of power could not take place during the war, the ministries in the eight Congress provinces resigned. This decision has often been criticized, but the Congress leadership recognized that if they continued in office, they would be forced to cooperate with the British, and powerful factions within the Congress itself would use this cooperation to undermine their authority. The threat to the leadership came from two main sources : the communists, who in the early stages of the war had denounced it as imperialist aggression and Subhas Chandra Bose and his followers, who were willing to cooperate with the Germans in return for help in overthrowing the British. Bose and his followers thought the time had come when the nationalist movement would finally move to a direct, and, if necessary, violent, confrontation with the British. The German triumphs in Europe in the spring and summer of 1940 had set the stage. Bose wrote :

As every day passes one feels like biting his fingers in helpless agony. Can nothing be done to save India even at this late hour? Will not the enslaved people of India cast off their lethargy . . . and stand up as one man to demand liberty. . . . When Europe is in the melting pot, who can withstand the demand of three hundred and fifty millions of Indians.[1]

When the British refused the Congress' demand for an immediate establishment of an independent government, they argued that this was impossible not only because of the war, but also because they "could not contemplate transfer of their present responsibilities for the peace and welfare of India to any system of government whose authority is directly denied by large and powerful elements in India's national life."[2] What they had in mind, of course, was the Muslim League, and they were thus in effect giving a veto over constitutional change to Jinnah and the Muslim League.

Two-Nation Concept

Jinnah, who up to this time had been struggling to make the Muslim League politically significant, became the spokesman for the Muslims. In future negotiations he did not have to state his aims nor did he have to prove that he spoke for all, or even a majority, of Indian Muslims. His strength was the British insistence that the rights of all minorities be safeguarded.

Although Jinnah did not offer any concrete proposals for constitutional change at this time, he further refined the concept of Muslim nationalism. The only hope for a reasonable life for Muslims was the recognition that Hindus and Muslims constituted two nations. This view found formal expression in a resolution of the Muslim League at Lahore in March 1940.

No constitutional plan would be workable in this country or acceptable to the Muslims unless it is designated on the following basic principles, viz., that geographically contiguous units are demarcated into regions that should be so constituted . . . that the areas in which the Muslims are numerically in a majority as in the North-Western ahd Eastern zones should be

grouped to constitute "Independent States" in which the constituent units shall be autonomous and sovereign.[3]

This was a more precise definition of Iqbal's idea of Muslim
provinces, to which the name of "Pakistan," from the initial letters
of the various Muslim majority areas, had been given by an Indian
Muslim student at Cambridge in 1933. There was still much ambiguity about what Jinnah really meant, whether he was thinking of
two separate Muslim states—one in what is now West Pakistan,
the other East Bengal—or if he meant by "states" merely provinces
with a large measure of autonomy. But he had given at least a
minimal statement of his goal. The idea that Hindus and Muslims
could ever evolve a common nationality was, he said at this time,
a dream that failed to see that Hindus and Muslims drew their inspiration for nationhood from different sources of history.

The Muslim League's vitality came simply from opposing the
Indian National Congress, but the Congress had to have a program to maintain its popular support. In Bengal Bose's Forward
Bloc was winning adherents through its undeviating opposition to
the British. In northern India many Hindus, including Congressmen,
dismayed at the growing power of the Muslim League, were convinced that the Congress, by refusing to cooperate with the British,
had played into Jinnah's hands. They were also disenchanted with
nonviolence, especially as there were renewed outbreaks of Hindu-
Muslim rioting in which, the Hindus believed, the Muslims had been
the aggressors. K. M. Munshi, one of the most prominent Congressmen and a close friend of Gandhi, expressed a widespread view
when he spoke of the "planned Communal frenzy" directed by the
Muslim League against Hindu women and children and of how he
"boiled with rage at our impotence" in not fighting back.[4]

Allied Pressure

Tension increased after the entrance of Japan into the war at
the end of 1941. The rapid advance of the Japanese through
Southeast Asia forced all groups to face the prospect of an immi-
nent Japanese invasion. A new factor in the situation was the
pressure put on Britain at this time by her allies, China and the
United States, to gain India's full support for the war effort by
meeting some of the nationalist demands for an immediate move

toward granting independence. This was the first time that the Indian nationalists had received any substantial backing from foreign governments. Unlike earlier national movements in Europe and later ones in Asia and Africa, Indian nationalism had few debts to outside political forces.

The Chinese nationalist leader, Chiang Kai-shek, who had been in touch with Nehru at the outbreak of the war, visited India in February 1942 and became convinced that unless the British made some move, Indians would not resist the Japanese. The United States government had already raised the question of Indian independence with Churchill, reflecting pressure from groups in the United States that had long been sympathetic with the Indian cause. And the fall of Singapore made the matter more urgent. Setting up a temporary dominion government of India, Roosevelt urged Churchill, "might cause the people there to forget hard feelings"[5] and to join wholeheartedly in the war against Japan. Some interpreters have suggested that the American intervention was the prime influence in persuading Churchill to open negotiations with the Indian political leaders by sending Sir Stafford Cripps to India. This suggestion is doubtful since there was strong support for such action from the Labour members of the British government, but it may well have been one of the deciding factors.

Cripps mission

Cripps arrived in India in March 1942, bringing with him the British government's proposal that as soon as the war was over steps would be taken to set up in India an elected body to frame a constitution for a new Indian union. This would "constitute a Dominion associated with the United Kingdom and other Dominions by common allegiance to the Crown but equal to them in every respect." Any province that wished to remain outside this Indian union would have the right to do so and would be given the same status as the Indian union. Meanwhile the government would invite the immediate participation of the leaders of the Indian people in the running of the country. The task of "organizing to the full the military, moral and material resources of India must be the responsibility of the Government of India," with the British government retaining "control, and direction, of the defense of India as part of their world war effort."[6]

The promise of the Cripps mission that Britain would give India her freedom when the war ended was, in words attributed to Gandhi, "a blank cheque on a failing bank." The Indian National Congress leaders were interested only in what Britain had to offer immediately, and when the proposals were examined, this was found to be very little. All the essential powers were to be left with the governor general and the commander in chief of the army ; the Indians would find their role through an effective prosecution of the war. There was little reason why the Congress leaders should have been willing to consider this proposal.

One aspect of the proposal made it particularly unacceptable : the statement that a province could, in effect, secede from the Indian union. As a concession to the Muslim League, this meant that the Congress would agree in advance to the partition of the country. Jinnah and the Muslim League did not have to press their position ; as in the past and as it was to be later on, all that was necessary to wait, leaving the action to the Congress. Jinnah knew, as responsible British opinion might have known, that such a proposition was unthinkable to the Congress in 1942. Events finally forced its acceptance in 1947, but in 1942 among the Congress leaders only Rajagopalachari urged that the Muslim League's demands should even be recognized as negotiable. The nation they envisaged was coterminous with the Indian Empire the British had created.

The British insistence on their responsibility to protect minorities had now become a dogma with them, the full implications of which were in fundamental conflict with the Congress' commitment to a united India under a parliamentary democracy. The Muslims were not, of course, the only minority. The Depressed Classes under Dr. Ambedkar's leadership had denounced Cripps' proposals, believing they threatened to return the untouchables to "the black days of the ancient past" by placing them "under an unmitigated system of Hindu rule."[7] In addition, religious minorities, such as the Sikhs and Christians, were also concerned for their future. But in 1942 only the Muslims were in a position to profit from British concern, and it was Churchill's concentration on the Muslims that made genuine negotiations impossible. When Churchill heard that Cripps had failed, he is said literally to have danced with joy. The failure justified his view that the divisions within Indian life made the continuance of British rule inevitable.

"Quit India" Resolution

After the failure of the Cripps mission the Congress leaders had to show that Churchill's interpretation of Indian nationalism was wrong. This could only be done by an unmistakable response from the Indian people, and for this they turned once more to Gandhi. His answer was a new civil disobedience campaign. Because of the war, with its threat of invasion, the implications of such a course of action were far different from what they had been before. Gandhi's age—he was now 73—and his long experience with nonviolent movements might have made him cautious, but in fact he moved to more extreme positions. Before, he had always counseled careful preparation before starting a campaign, but now he believed that neither he nor the nation had much time. He realized that the result might be anarchy, for he no longer had any illusions about the ability of ordinary people to follow the way of nonviolence. But he was willing to take the risk. Nor did he fear a Japanese invasion. All that mattered was that the Indian people, without help from anyone, British or Japanese, should seize their own future. "That is why," he said, "I have made up my mind that it would be a good thing if a million people were shot in a brave and non-violent rebellion against the British rule." His friends and opponents were equally shocked by this argument, but he brushed them aside, saying, "they do not know the fire that is raging in my breast."[8]

The result of Gandhi's resumption of leadership was the "Quit India" resolution passed by the Indian National Congress at Bombay on August 8, 1942. As in 1920 there were very few of the leaders who accepted his course wholeheartedly, but they had no alternative to propose to either his passion or his logic. The long resolution demanded the immediate withdrawal of British power from India since "the continuation of that rule is degrading and enfeebling India, and making her progressively less capable of defending herself." Gandhi gave India a *mantra*, a sacred formula.

The mantra is : Do or Die. We shall either free India or die in the attempt; we shall not live to see the perpetuation of

our slavery. . . . Take a pledge with God and your own conscience as witness, that you will no longer rest till freedom is
achieved and will be prepared to lay down your lives in the
attempt to achieve it.[9]

Once more Gandhi had become the apotheosis of the nation.
His old opponent, Subhas Chandra Bose, who had by this time
joined the Japanese, rejoiced that Gandhi had at last seen what he
himself had long preached, that "the destruction of British power
in India was the *sine qua non* for the solution of all India's
problems." The Congress' resolution, he was convinced, expressed
"the wish of the vast majority of the Indian people."[10]

The government was in no mood in the summer of 1942 to
wait as it had in 1922 and 1930. Within a few hours of the passing of the resolution, all the leaders were arrested and imprisoned;
the Congress was declared an illegal organization ; its newspapers
were closed ; and its funds were confiscated.

After the arrests of the Congress leaders, India was swept
during August and September by a wave of violence unmatched
since 1857. Students took the initiative in the early stages, leading
processions through the streets, overturning cars and buses, and
forcing the shopkeepers to close their stores. Then a second
phase began with attacks on government property throughout the
country, but especially in the United Provinces and Bihar, the
strongholds of the Congress. Hundreds of railway stations, post
offices, and other government offices were attacked and damaged.
Next came a wave of sabotage, in which telegraph wires were cut
and railway bridges and tracks were blown up. This was so successful in Bihar that for some time Bengal was cut off from all
communication with the rest of India. Large areas in rural Bihar
and Bengal ceased to be controlled by the government as the
peasants destroyed records and chased out officials.

The Indian historian R.C. Majumdar was hardly overstating
the situation when he wrote that "as soon as Gandhi and his
followers were removed to prison, the cult of non-violence, as
understood and preached by them, came to an end, nevermore to
figure as a potent force in India's struggle for freedom."[11] There
was, however, no master strategy for all of India, or at least none
that could be put into operation, and even in a single region there
might be a number of groups working independently. Perhaps

the most effective leadership came from the socialists, whose leader, Jayprakash Narayan, escaped from jail to organize underground resistance. Followers of the old revolutionary parties in Bengal and elsewhere, who had never accepted the Gandhian ideology, also took part in acts of sabotage.

The uprisings of August 1942 had another important result : the further polarization of the Muslim League's position. For Jinnah the "Quit India" resolution was one more example of Gandhi's method of nonviolence leading to a breakdown of law and order, but he was unwilling to take a very strong public stand lest this might antagonize the Hindus, who might then turn on the Muslims. A cautious neutrality was therefore observed by the Muslim League, but even so, in areas of Bihar and Bengal the riots of 1942 often had an anti-Muslim tinge. The Hindu Mahasabha, while opposing Gandhi, made much of the League's failure to support the nationalist cause and called the agitation for a separate Muslim state "outrageous and treacherous."[12]

The dilemma of Indian nationalism was dramatized by Gandhi in 1944, when, after his release from prison because of ill health, he met for a long series of discussions with Jinnah. The basis for the talks was the League's demand for a separate state, and Gandhi seemed willing to go a long way toward making concessions. But what he could not concede was the heart of Jinnah's position : the acknowledgement that India contained two nations, one Muslim, one Hindu. In denying this proposition Gandhi rather surprisingly argued that since foreign rule had united India politically, the only lawful test of Indian nationhood was the fact that all the racial and religious groups had been brought under a common political subjection. "If you and I throw off this subjection by our combined effort", he pleaded with Jinnah, "we shall be born a politically free nation."[12] Gandhiji's appeal to a concept of nationhood grounded on the historical fact of a political unity created by a foreign power and looking to a future based in a common struggle for freedom from that power was ingenious. But essentially it was a solution that ignored the existence of a Muslim nationality created by the very success of the Indian National Congress. Jinnah had already crystallized the inchoate fears and aspirations of India's Muslims into another nationalist expression.

Negotiations for Independence

The long-drawn-out negotiations for a settlement began in June 1945 with the governor general, Lord Wavell, bringing together the leaders of the Indian National Congress and the Muslim League to discuss the formation of a new Executive Council. Jinnah's insistence that all the Muslims who were nominated should be members of the League was irreconcilable with the Congress' position that religion was not a factor in political representation. But the real difficulty was that neither the League nor the Congress was much interested in interim proposals. Then with the victory of the Labour party in the British elections in July and the end of the war in August came a change in the political climate. The Labour party was anxious to settle the Indian question, partly because of its old commitments to Indian freedom, but more urgently because its priorities demanded the expenditure of its energies on social change at home, not in holding on to India.

As a preliminary step toward forming a constitutional assembly, elections were held in India in September 1945, for the first time since 1937. The results confirmed the changes that had been apparent in the interval. The Indian National Congress maintained its unchallenged control of all the general seats, and the Muslim League, which had done poorly in 1937, won 446 out of the 495 seats reserved for Muslims. After the election Congress governments took power in eight provinces ; the League took concontrol in two ; and a coalition, including Muslim groups that opposed the League, took control of the Punjab.

With popularly elected ministries in office once more in the provinces, the British government sent a Cabinet mission to India in March 1946 to negotiate the transfer of power. The plan that the Cabinet mission brought with them envisaged the creation of an Indian union, in which the central government would have control of foreign affairs, defense, and communications, and the provinces would be left the other powers. The provinces would be formed into three groups, each of which would have separate executive and legislative bodies. This grouping of provinces was intended to satisfy the Muslim League without conceding the establishment of a separate state. There would be one group, made up of the Punjab, the North-West Frontier Province, and Sind, which would have a Muslim majority.

The plan was the subject of intense negotiation during the summer of 1946. There were two basic constitutional issue at stake : first, whether there should be a strong central government or a relatively weak one, with most of the power developing to the provinces, including the right of secession ; second, whether the constitution would provide for the continued special electoral representation for religious and other minority groups. On these two issues the Congress and the League had fundamentally different views that were the product of the roles that each had played in the development of nationalism in India. The irreconcilability of these views was marked by the acceptance, with many reservations, of the general scheme of the Cabinet mission plan by both the League and the Congress.

At this point, when agreement seemed to be in sight, Jawaharlal Nehru, as president of the Indian National Congress, declared that although the Congress members were entering the constituent assembly under the rules laid down by the Cabinet mission, once the assembly met they would not be bound any longer by British rules. "What we do there we are entirely and absolutely free to determine."[13] Jinnah immediately denounced Nehru's position as "a complete repudiation of the basic form upon which the long-term scheme rests."[14] A few days later the Muslim League withdrew its previous acceptance of the Cabinet mission plan and reasserted the League's adherence to a separate state of Pakistan as the only possible solution of the problem of Muslim survival.

The most influential Muslim in the Congress, Maulana Azad, has called Nehru's statement "one of those unfortunate events that change the course of history."[15] It completed the process of alienating Jinnah that Nehru had begun with his refusal to include the representatives of the League in the provincial governments in 1937. But speeches do not often change the course of history, and what Nehru had done was to express a political reality. An Indian nation had been brought into being, and it would have been impossible to circumscribe the freedom of the members of the constituent assembly by the commitments of the Cabinet plan. As for the League, Nehru's speech freed them from a position to which they had never really given wholehearted assent. From this time on the partition of India became the central fact of political life, although the Congress leaders continued during the next few months to express their unyielding objection to it.

Meanwhile, there were signs that the disorders that many feared would follow the end of British rule had already begun. Hindu-Muslim riots raged in Calcutta during August 1946, leaving at least three thousand dead and many thousands more injured and homeless. The Muslim League has been blamed for the Calcutta killings, since they began on August 16, the day the League had called for "Direct Action" in the form of strikes and rallies against the Congress, but in the end, as a minority in the great city, it was the Muslim community that suffered the most. Reprisals against Muslims also followed in Bihar and East Bengal.

Even more ominous for the government was the mutiny that had broken out in the navy earlier in the year. There were also indications that the tensions between Hindus and Muslims in the civilian population were being transferred to the police and army. It was doubtful if the government could control the situation much longer, even if it had the will to use force. Both the Labour government in Great Britain and the British officials in India wanted to move quickly toward a solution, and Prime Minister Attlee's statement in the House of Commons on February 20, 1947, signaled the end of British rule.

> The present state of uncertainty is fraught with danger and cannot be indefinitely prolonged. His Majesty's Govenment wish to make it clear that it is their definite intention to effect the transference of power to responsible Indian hands by a date not later than June, 1948.[16]

Lord Louis Mountbatten was appointed governor general to carry out this program.

Partition

In referring to "responsible Indian hands," Attlee was using the language common to British constitutional statements on India since 1909, but now a time limit had been set and the alternatives were stated. There were three possibilities for a transfer of power : It could be given to a government of a united India, as agreed by the political parties ; to existing provinicial governments ; or "in

some other way as may seem most reasonable and in the best interests of the Indian people."[17] As Jinnah had long recognized, the
choice was up to Indian National Congress. The Muslim League had
a veto over transferring power to a united government, for they
could demand a price the Congress would be unwilling to pay—a
weak central government. The second possibility, the transfer of
power to the provinces, means the creation of perhaps a dozen
autonomous states, not counting the hundreds of princely states
that would also become independent. Such a choice went against
the whole development of Indian nationhood which the Congress
had fostered. The third possibility, concealed in the phrase
"some other way as may seem most reasonable", meant, in effect,
agreeing to the creation of Pakistan, an idea the Congress leaders
had always refused to take seriously. It had now become the most
realistic of the choices.

The acceptance of partition by the Indian National Congress
leaders was a wrenching decision. It was a denial of the Congress'
creed that Indian nationalism was not determined by religious
affiliation, but by a common culture that transcended religious
differences. Partition was an admission of failure, a tacit acknow-
ledgment of the old argument that India was not a nation. The
success of the nationalist movement in creating a self-conscious
awareness of Indian nationhood made the trauma of partition all
the deeper. This was as true for those with a secular vision of
India as for those whose perception was deeply colored by religious imagery and passion, who instinctively equated political India
as it was when it had came into existence in the nineteenth century
with *Bharat Mata*, or Mother India, the holy land of Hindu myth
and legend. More than any other religion in the world, Hinduism
is bound up with a holy geography, for there is hardly a river or
mountain not associated with some event in the sacred literature.
And this motherland was being divided.

In the whole complex of issues involved in partition and the
actual transfer of power from British to Indian hands, the dominant figure was Sardar Patel, not Nehru or Gandhi. Patel had
been important in nationalist politics since the early 1920s, but his
concern with party organization had not given him the public fame
of the other leaders. Now his skills brought him to the forefront,
and when he became convinced that partition was the best solution
for the impasse, he carried his colleagues with him. His knowledge

of Indian regional politics convinced him that throughout the country there were forces at work that would lead to disruption, so that India would be faced with the prospect of not one partition, but many, unless a strong central government took over. Partition was a blow to the dreams of Indian nationalists, but Patel's acceptance of it exacted a heavy price from Jinnah and the League : the partition of Bengal and Punjab. The League had claimed the whole of both provinces as the very heartland of the Pakistan idea. Jinnah would get Pakistan, but it would be, as he said, a "moth-eaten" one. Thirty million Muslims remained in India. There was thus no great triumph in his victory. He was also conscious that many Hindus accepted Pakistan as a way of getting rid of a large number of Muslims, thus making India more truely a Hindu state.

In the end Patel carried even Gandhi to an unwilling recognition that partition was the only practical course, given the attitude of both the Indian National Congress and the Muslim League. This did not mean that Gandhi gave his approval to the Congress' decision in June 1947 to accept partition ; he only acknowledged that he had become "a back number" and that the leaders of the Congress were not with him. According to his biographer, Pyarelal, henceforth "the impossible old man was put on the pedestal, admired for his genius . . . listened to with respectful attention and bypassed."[18] Yet Gandhi did not cease to be what he had been for nearly thirty years, the one acknowledged symbol of the potential of Indian nationality, which was as complex and ambiguous as his words and actions. Nothing proved this ambiguity more clearly than his death seven months later at the hands of Hindus who regarded him as the betrayer of India.

The British government had set June 1948 as the deadline for the transfer of power, but after his arrival in India in the spring of 1947, Lord Mountbatten became convinced that the existing administration, the uneasy alliance of Indian leaders with the British government, should not attempt to hold power for more than a few months. He therefore announced early in June that the transfer of power would take place on August 15, 1947, a year earlier than had been planned. British power in India had been legitimized by its ability to maintain law and order and by the tacit acceptance of the people ; now both these sources of authority were rapidly being eroded. As violence spread throughout north India

the soldiers and police, the ultimate guarantee of British power in
India for nearly two hundred years, became increasingly unreliable
instruments of the administration. There was uneasiness among
all the classes whose fortunes had been linked with the British : the
commercial and professional groups, the industrialists, the landlords, the princes. The British themselves, the administrators and
soldiers, were anxious to end their part in the long drama and go
home. The basic decision was that power would devolve to two
central governments; the existing provinces of Bengal and Punjab
would be partitioned so that the areas where Muslims were in a
majority would go to Pakistan and those with a majority of non-
Muslims would go to India.

*   *   *

When the formal transfer of power to the two governments,
India and Pakistan, took place on August 15, 1947, it was acknowledged that the new dominion of India was the successor state to the
old government of India, continuing, as the secretary of state put it,
"the international personality of existing India". As for Pakistan,
the United Nations decided it was "part of an existing state breaking off to form a new State."[19] The legal phraseology neatly sum-
marized the search for nationhood and nationality that defined the
modern political history of the subcontinent of India. Just before
the separation of the states became final, Nehru had told the
constituent assembly in Delhi, "Long years ago we made a tryst
with destiny, and now the time comes when we shall reedeem our
pledge." He had in mind the coming of India's independence, but
the tryst with destiny had included the creation of not one
nationality, but two. And among the pledges that had to be
redeemed after August 15 were the prophecies that had long been
made that the withdrawal of British power would be followed by
violence and chaos. There were two months of bloodshed as the
two nations that had been created out of a common past pulled
themselves apart. Gandhi, who had been so central to the whole
process as a symbol and a catalyst, now turned away in despair,
praying for an end to his life so that he would not have to
be a "helpless witness of the butchery by man become savage."[20]
But by the end of 1947 the worst of the violence was over, and

the two nations recovered their stability, fulfilling the final test of nationhood, the capacity to survive.

There are, however, four general principles that can be identified as part of India's nationalist ideology. First of all is the consensus, rooted in the history of the nationalist movement, that the preservation of the unity of India takes precedence over all other commitments. An emphasis on the importance of national unity runs through the speeches and writing of India's leaders in a way that would be hard to match in any other country. The sources of this concern for unity have been frequently mentioned in this essay. One was the reiteration by the British that Indian unity was an artifact of imperial power and would not survive their departure, coupled with a recognition on the part of some thoughtful leaders that India is indeed, in some fashion, what she was called in the Montagu-Chelmsford Report, "a sisterhood of states", something in fact new under the political sun. This means that nationality is understood primarily in territorial terms, and not as in the case of Pakistan, in an ideology that is in a curious sense not related to territory. India's national identity has instead as a fundamental referent a territorial base, that is, areas over which India assumed sovereignty in 1957, or which had accrued to her since, by legal or historical right, as in the case of Goa and Kashmir. The stress on nationality as a function of territorial sovereignty of a people deriving their identity from a defined territory is the basis of most nationlism, at least in the West, and it surely constitutes a source of political and social stability. Another item of the national consensus is the conviction that the Government had a primary responsibility for ameliorating the poverty of the masses. The former rulers of of India had frequently enough proclaimed—and probably quite genuinely—their concern for the Indian masses, but in post-independence India there was a conviction, unlike under the imperial regime, that there must be radical and widespread social change. This belief in the necessity of social change, and duty of government to promote it, is probably one of the crucial differences between imperial ond post-imperial rule. There is a wide divergence between the rhetoric of rulers and their actual intentions, not to speak of their achievements, but in India, as in most of the countries that have achieved political independence from colonial rule since 1947, a sense of national identity carries with it a longing for economic betterment. The preservation of national unity and the movement towards economic justice are set in the context of third element in the national consensus in India. That is the apparently widespread acceptance that a multi-party democracy is peculiarly relevant to the traditions and ethos of the Indian people. The survival of political democracy is surely a reflection of the sense of national identity that was forged in the pre-independence period, as well as one of the factors that continues to maintain it.

A fourth component of the nationalism of modern India is the conviction that India must be given her rightful place in the comity of nations. This demand for a place in the sun did not play as central a role in Indian nationalism as it did in the history of European nationalism, but it has surely been of great importance since 1947. India's sense of nationhood carries with it a demand for recognition that is commensurate with its history, its human resources, and potential for leadership.

In the last decades of the twentieth century, the environment for the development of nationalism in the sub-continent has altered drastically from the decades before Independence. In the nineteenth century and on through the first half of the twentieth, India was of very great importance in the world balance of power—far more so than her dependent political status would suggest. But it was a role masked and distorted by imperial connection as well as by the political and econonmic conditions of whole of Asia and the Middle East. European expansion from the seventeenth century onwards had given the sub-continent linkages with the world economic and political order that had developed with a European centre.

Power alignments since 1947 have given India an entirely different set of economic and political linkages from those that had existed previously. Linkages with Britain are far less important, for example, than those that many former French colonies have with France. This partly reflects the great resources of India in relation to Britain as well, of course, as the fact that Britain's departure from India coincided with a diminution of her role as a world power. Along with this must be mentioned a fact that often seems odd to foreign observers, namely, the friendly attitude towards Great Britain that existed after 1947. Thus when Mountbatten, the last of the imperial rulers was assassinated, India observed a period of mourning that one might have thought would have been reserved for a great national figure.

Almost immediately after 1947, India's foreign relations shifted their focus from Europe to the two great non-European powers, the United States and the Soviet Union. Neither had played a role in the independence movement, except for somewhat peripheral roles—the United States through pressures exerted on the British in relation to the war effort, and the Soviet Union through the ideological model it supplied to some of the nationalist leaders. India's relations with the great super powers have probably obscured the importance of other new linkages that developed after independence. One set of these was with China, with which India had had remarkably little contact since ancient times when Buddhism had been a medium of transposing Indian intellectual concepts to China. One of the important by-products of European imperialism was that it distorted relations between the Asian countries so that India had little contact in the nineteenth century with any of the other areas of East and South East Asia. India's intellectual life, as well as its economic patterns, were oriented towards western culture in many ways during the nineteenth century, and renewed contacts with the great civilizations of Asia will surely lead towards changes in India's cultural and intellectual life. But the truly new linkages in India's national life after 1947 came, paradoxically, with the other countries of the South Asian region—Pakistan, Nepal, Bangladesh, and Sri Lanka. The areas that are now Pakistan and Bangladesh had both been integral parts of previous Indian empires, and the cultures of Nepal and Sri Lanka have been deeply influenced by Indian sources. As independent soverign nations, they posed new issues for India, for during the formative phase of Indian nationalism there had been no genuinely independent nations on the borders of India. Thus in 1947 India found itself as the successor state of the old Government of India in terms of all its internal political and administrative structures but also as the legatee of its foreign policy in the area. This meant having to do what the British government had not had to do in India—come to terms with a ring of sovereign states. All of these relationships with the outside world built upon the national identity forged out of the richness and complexity of India's historical experience.

NOTES

[1]Bose, *Crossroads*, pp. 292-293.

[2]Great Britain, *Parliamentary Papers*, 1939-1940, Vol. 10, Cmd. 6219, in Philips, *The Evolution of India and Pakistan*, p. 371.

[3]Quoted in Sayeed, *The Political System of Pakistan*, p. 40.

[4]K.M. Munshi, *Indian Constitutional Documents* (Bombay ; Bharatiya Vidya Bhavan, 1967), Vol. I, p. 86.

[5]R.C. Majumdar, *History of the Freedom Movement* (Calcutta : Firma K.L. Mukhopadhyay, 1963), Vol. III, p. 619.

[6]"Draft Proposals," quoted in V.P. Menon, *The Transfer of Power in India* (New Delhi : Orient Longmans, 1968), p. 124.

[7]Quoted in R. Coupland, *Indian Politics* 1936-1942 (London ; Oxford University Press, 1944), p. 280.

[8]Quoted in Tendulkar, *Mahatma*, Vol. VI, p. 137.

[9]*Ibid.*, p. 161.

[10]Subhas Chandra Bose, *The Indian Struggle* (Bombay : Asia Publishing House, 1964), p. 350.

[11]Majumdar, *History of the Freedom Movement*, Vol. III, p. 646.

[12]Quoted in Tendulkar, *Mahatma*, Vol. VI, p. 277.

[13]Quoted in Menon, *Transfer of Power*, p. 283.

[14]*Ibid.*, p. 284.

[15]A.K. Azad, *India Wins Freedom* (Bombay : Orient Longmans, 1959), p. 154.

[16]Statement by Prime Minister Attlee, February 20, 1920, quoted in Menon, *Transfer of Power*, Appendix IX.

[17]*Ibid.*

[18]Pyarelal, *Mahatma Gandhi, the Last Phase* (Ahmedabad : Navajivan Publishing House, 1958, Vol. II, p. 153.

[19]Quoted in Menon, *Transfer of Power*, pp. 412-413.

[20]Quoted in Tendulkar, *Mahatma*, Vol. VIII, p. 145.

Bibliographical Note

For bibliographical information on works in English on almost all aspects of Indian history the most useful source is Maureen L. P. Patterson, editor, *South Asian Civilizations: A Bibliographical Synthesis*, (Chicago: University of Chicago Press, 1981). Joseph E. Schwartzberg, editor, *A Historical Atlas of South Asia*, (Chicago: University of Chicago Press, 1978), has detailed maps on territorial changes as well as much information on languages, religions, economics, etc. *Sources of Indian Tradition*, revised edition edited by Ainslie T. Embree and Stephen Hay, 2 vols., (New York : Columbia University Press, 1988), has a representative selection in Vol. 2 from the writings of most of the leading figures associated with the nationalist movement. For Indian history as a whole, Romila Thapar and Percival Spear, *A History of India* (London and Baltimore: Penguin, 1968) is both readable and reliable. The older work by R.C. Majumbar, H.C. Raychaudhuri and K.K. Datta, *An Advanced History of India* (London: Macmillan, 1960) is very useful for its wealth of factual details, as is Vincent Smith, *Oxford History of India*, revised by Percival Spear (Oxford : Clarendon Press, 1967). Stanley Wolpert, *A New History of India* (Oxford and New York : Oxford University Press, 1982) gives useful survey of most aspects of Indian history, with selected bibliographical notes for all the main topics. Judith Brown, *Modern India : The Origins of a Social Democracy* (Oxford and New York: Oxford University Press, 1985) takes into account all the most recent historiographical work on modern India, and the "Suggestions for Further Reading" is an excellent guide to current scholarship on the nationalist period.

Chapter 1 : One Great Nation ?
   Census of India, 1891 : *General Report*. London ; H.M.S.O., 1893.

Davis, Kingsley. *The Population of India and Pakistan.* Princeton, N.J. : Princeton University Press, 1951.

*Deutsch, Karl W. *Nationalism and Social Communication.* Cambridge : Massachusetts Institute of Technology Press, 1967.

*Kohn, Hans. *The Idea of Nationalism.* New York : Macmillan, 1944.

*Pye, Lucian. *Politics, Personality, and Nation Building.* New Haven, Conn : Yale University Press, 1968.

Report on the Census of British India, 1881, 3 vols. London : H.M.S.O., 1883.

Chapter 2 : Voices of India

Ahmad, Aziz. *Islamic Modernism in India and Pakistan, 1857-1964.* London : Oxford University Press, 1967.

Gopal, S. *The Vice-Royalty of Lord Ripon.* London : Oxford University Press, 1953.

McCully, B.T. *English Education and the Origin of Indian Nationalism.* New York : Columbia University Press, 1940.

Majumdar, B.B. *Indian Political Associations and Reform of Legislature (1818-1917).* Calcutta : Firma K.L. Mukhopadhyay, 1965.

Martin, Briton. *New India 1885.* Berkeley : University of California Press, 1969.

Seal Anil. *Emergence of Indian Nationalism.* Cambridge : University Press, 1968.

Wolpert, Stanley. *Tilak and Gokhale.* Berkeley : University of California Press, 1961.

Chapter 3 : Search for a Center

Chandra, Bipin. *The Rise and Growth of Economic Nationalism in India.* New Delhi : People's Publishing Company, 1966.

Great Britain. *Parliamentary Papers,* 1918, Vol. 8., Cd. 9109, "The Montagu-Chelmsford Report."

Koss, Stephen. *John Morley at the India Office.* New Haven, Conn : Yale University Press, 1969.

---

*Available in paperback.

Majumdar, B.B. *Militant Nationalism in India.* Calcutta : General Printers, 1966.

Wasti, Syed Razi. *Lord Minto and the Indian Nationalists.* Oxford : Clarendon Press, 1964.

Chapter 4 : The Emergence of Gandhi

Broomfield, John. *Elite Conflict in a Plural Society.* Berkeley : University of California Press, 1968.

*Erikson, Erik. *Gandhi's Truth.* New York : Norton, 1969.

Nanda, B.R. *Mahatma Gandhi.* London : Allen & Unwin, 1958.

Tendulkar, D.G. *Mahatma.* 8 vols. New Delhi : Publications Division, Government of India, 1960-1962.

Chapter 5 : The Politics of Right Mistakes

Dwarkadas, Kanji. *India's Fight for Freedom.* Bombay : Popular Prakashan, 1966.

Gopal, S. *The Vice-Royalty of Lord Irwin.* Oxford : Clarendon Press, 1957.

Irschick, Eugene. *Politics and Social Conflict in South India.* Berkeley : University of California Press, 1969.

Majumdar, S.K. *Jinnah and Gandhi.* Calcutta : Firma K.L. Mukhopadhyay, 1966.

*Nehru Jawaharlal. *An Autobiography.* Bombay : Allied Publishers, 1962.

*Sayeed, Kahild B. *The Political System of Pakistan.* Boston : Houghton Mifflin, 1967.

Chapter 6 : End and Beginning

Azad, A.K. *India Wins Freedom.* Bombay : Orient Longmans, 1959.

Brecher, Michael, *Nehru : A Political Biography.* London : Oxford University Press, 1959.

Majumdar, R.C. *History of the Freedom Movement,* Vol. III. Calcutta : Firma K.L. Mukhopadhyay, 1963.

Menon, V.P. *The Transfer of Power in India.* Princeton, N.J. : Princeton University Press, 1957.

Munshi, K.M. *Indian Constitutional Documents.* 2 Vols. Bombay : Bharatiya Vidya Bhavan, 1967.

Rudolph, Lloyd I., and Susanne H. *The Modernity of Tradition.* Chicago : University of Chicago Press, 1967.

Chronology

1880-1884	Lord Ripon, governor general
1884	Ilbert Bill controversy
1885	Indian National Congress founded
1889-1905	Lord Curzon, governor general
1896-1900	Years of plague and famine
1905	Partition of Bengal
1906	Muslim League founded
1907	Moderate-extremist clash at Surat Congress
1909	Morley-Minto Reforms
1916	Lucknow Pact between Muslim League and Indian National Congress
1917	Announcement by British Parliament promising responsible government
1919	Montagu-Chelmsford Reforms ; Rowlatt Acts ; Amritsar massacre
1920	Khilafat movement ; noncooperation adopted by Indian National Congress under M.K. Gandhi's leadership
1921	Inauguration of new constitutional reforms
1922	Abortive civil disobedience movement ; end of noncooperation movement
1923	Swaraj party formed
1928	Simon Commission
1929	Indian National Congress declares complete independence its goal
1930-1931	Civil disobedience movement
1932	Award of communal seats in legislative assemblies
1932-1934	Civil disobedience movement
1935	Government of India Act
1937	Responsible government in provinces
1939	Resignation of Congress ministries
1940	Muslim League demand for separate state
1942	Cripps mission, "Quit India" resolution ; Indian National Congress leaders jailed

1944   British begin negotiations for independence ; elections held

1946   Cabinet mission ; interim government formed

December 9, 1946   Constituent Assembly convened

1947   Lord Mountbatten, governor general ; announcement of plans for partition of India

August 15, 1947   Independence of India and Pakistan ; Nehru, Prime Minister of India ; Jinnah governor general of Pakistan

Index